Ghost Hunter's Guide
to
Monterey and
California's Central
Coast

ter's Guide
to
Monterey and California's Central Coast

Jeff Dwyer

PELICAN PUBLISHING COMPANY
GRETNA 2010

*The word "Pelican" and the depiction of a pelican are trademarks
of Pelican Publishing Company, Inc., and are registered in the
U.S. Patent and Trademark Office.*

Library of Congress Cataloging-in-Publication Data

Dwyer, Jeff.
  Ghost hunter's guide to Monterey and California's central coast / Jeff Dwyer.
    p. cm.
  Includes index.
  ISBN 978-1-58980-809-6 (pbk. : alk. paper) 1. Haunted places—
California—Monterey Bay Region—Guidebooks. 2. Ghosts—California—
Monterey Bay Region. 3. Haunted places—California—Pacific Coast—
Guidebooks. 4. Ghosts—California—Pacific Coast. 5. Monterey Bay
Region (Calif.)—Guidebooks. 6. Pacific Coast (Calif.)—Guidebooks. 7.
Monterey Bay Region (Calif.)—History, Local. 8. Pacific Coast (Calif.)—
History, Local. I. Title.
  BF1472.U6D8675 2010
  133.109794'76—dc22
                                    2010019026

Printed in the United States of America

Published by Pelican Publishing Company, Inc.
1000 Burmaster Street, Gretna, Louisiana 70053

To my daughter, Sarah Shannon Dwyer

Contents

Acknowledgments

As always, I am indebted to my literary agent, Sue Janet Clark, for invaluable guidance and support, and endless patience. Also, my thanks go to Katie Szadziewicz and Heather Green of Pelican Publishing Company for invaluable assistance in promoting and editing my books.

I wish to thank my ghost-hunting colleagues, Norene Balovich and Jackie Ganiy, for their constant encouragement and interest in my work, and Loyd Auerbach, whose scholarship and writing have inspired and enlightened me. I am also grateful to my wife, Darlene, and children, Sam, Michael, and Sarah, for the good times that keep me going.

Introduction

Who believes in ghosts? People from every religion, culture, and generation believe that ghosts exist. The popularity of ghosts and haunted places in books, television programs, and movies reflects a belief held by many people that other dimensions and spiritual entities do exist.

In 2000, a Gallup poll discovered a significant increase in the number of Americans who believe in ghosts since the question was first asked in 1978. Thirty-one percent of respondents said they believed ghosts exist. In 1978, only 11 percent admitted to believing in ghosts. Less than a year later, in 2001, Gallup found that 42 percent of the public believed a house could be haunted, but only 28 percent believed that we can hear from or mentally communicate with someone who has died. A 2003 Harris poll found that an astounding 51 percent of Americans believed in ghosts. As with preceding polls, belief in ghosts was greatest among females. More young people accepted the idea of ghosts than older people. Forty-four percent of people aged 18 to 29 years admitted a belief in ghosts compared with 13 percent of those over 65. In 2005, a CBS News poll reported similar findings. Twenty-two percent of the respondents admitted they had personally seen or felt the presence of a ghost. In this same year, Gallup pollsters reported that 75 percent of Americans believed in at least one paranormal phenomenon, including ESP, reincarnation, spirit channeling, ghosts, and clairvoyance. More recently, in 2007, an Associated Press survey reported that 34 percent of Americans believed in ghosts.

Polls and surveys are interesting, but there is no way of knowing how many people have seen or heard a ghost only to feel too embarrassed, foolish, or frightened to admit it. Many ghost hunters and paranormal investigators believe a vast majority of people have seen or heard something from the other side, or spirit world, but failed to recognize it.

Today, many residents and visitors to California's central coast choose that destination because they believe that ghostly phenomena can be experienced there. This is evidenced by the increased popularity of tours of cemeteries, missions, and historic districts in the quaint towns and villages of the region and the number of paranormal investigations staged by local organizations.

Broadcast and cable television channels recognize the phenomenal nationwide interest in paranormal phenomena. The Syfy channel airs a weekly one-hour prime-time program called *Ghost Hunters.* The popularity of this show has been so great that a spin-off, *Ghost Hunters International,* also airs during prime time. Cast members of these documentary shows have achieved celebrity status. In December 2007, the Arts and Entertainment Channel premiered a new series called *Paranormal State* that follows a group of Pennsylvania State University students as they conduct investigations of ghosts and demons. The Travel Channel also offers two documentary programs that feature ghost investigations. *Most Haunted* follows a British cast of psychics, historians, and parapsychologists as they explore locations in the U.K. An American cast of three investigators is featured in *Ghost Adventures.* Discovery Channel and History Channel also offer documentary programs that often include dramatic re-creations of ghostly activity.

The major networks offer fact-based dramas that portray ghost encounters experienced by sensitives. CBS broadcasts a weekly primetime drama called *Medium* that follows the true-life experiences of psychic Allison Dubois of Arizona who communicates with ghosts in order to solve crimes. The network also produces the most popular show in this genre called *Ghost Whisperer,* which portrays the experiences of sensitive Mary Ann Winkowski of Ohio.

Internet users will find more than 3.5 million references to ghosts, ghost hunting, haunted places, and related paranormal phenomena. Search engines such as Google can aid ghost hunters in tracking down reports of ghostly activity in almost any city in America, locating paranormal investigative organizations they can join or consult, and purchasing ghost-hunting equipment or books that deal with the art and science of finding ghosts.

The recent worldwide interest in ghosts is not a spin-off of the New Age movement, the current popularity of angels, or the manifestation of some new religious process. The suspicion or recognition that ghosts exist is simply the reemergence of one of mankind's oldest and most basic beliefs: there is a life after death. Ancient writings from many cultures describe apparitions and a variety of spirit manifestations that include tolling bells, chimes, disembodied crying or moaning, and whispered messages. Legends and ancient books include descriptions of ghosts, dwelling places of spirits, and periods of intense spiritual activity related to seasons or community events such as festivals and crop harvests.

Vital interactions between the living and deceased have been described. Many ancient cultures included dead people or their spirits in community life. Spirits of the dead were sought as a source of guidance, wisdom, and protection for the living. Many followers of the worlds oldest religions agree that non-living entities may be contacted for guidance or may be seen on the earthly plane. Among these are visions of saints, the Virgin Mary, and angels.

Ancient sites of intense spiritual activity in Arizona, New Mexico, and Central and South America are popular destinations for travelers seeking psychic or spiritual experiences, as well as encounters with the paranormal. More modern, local sites where a variety of paranormal events have been documented are also popular destinations for adventurous living souls. Amateur and professional ghost hunters seek the spirits of the dearly departed in historic mansions, old theatres, pioneer-era bars and inns, firehouses, stores, and countless other places, including graveyards and famous hard rock mines. Modern buildings, city parks, restaurants and bars, numerous historic sites such as Colton Hall in Monterey, and seldom-traveled back country roads also serve as targets for ghost hunters.

Throughout the past two millennia, the popularity of the belief in ghosts has waxed and waned, similar to religious activity. When a rediscovery of ghosts and their role in our lives occurs, skeptics label the notion a fad or an aberration of modern lifestyles. Perhaps people are uncomfortable with the idea that ghosts exist because it involves an examination of our nature and our concepts of life, death, and afterlife. These concepts are most often considered in the context of religion, yet ghost hunters recognize that acceptance of the reality of ghosts, and a life after death, is a personal decision, having nothing to do with religious beliefs or church doctrine. An intellectual approach enables the ghost hunter to explore haunted places without religious bias or fear.

The great frequency of ghost manifestations on California's haunted coast, as evidenced by documentary reports on TV and other news media, reflects the success of amateur and professional ghost hunters who research and seek paranormal encounters in the region. Ghost hunting has become a popular weekend pastime for many adventurous souls, whether they are serious investigators or only causally interested in the paranormal. Advertisement of haunted inns, restaurants, and historical sites is commonplace. It is always fun, often very exciting, and may take ghost hunters places they had never dreamed of going.

ABOUT THIS BOOK

California's coastline spans 900 miles, comprising a large geographic area that cannot be covered in its entirety in this book. The central coast referred to in the title ranges from Moss Beach southward to Gaviota Beach near Santa Barbara. This region is often called the "haunted coast." In previous books, I wrote about other portions of the coast. *Ghost Hunter's Guide to California's Wine Country* includes Sonoma County and Mendocino County coastal regions. *Ghost Hunter's Guide to Los Angeles* includes haunted locations in Santa Barbara and Ventura, as well as several communities south of Los Angeles, including Long Beach and San Diego.

Chapter 1 of this book will help you, the ghost hunter, to research and organize your own ghost hunt at locations within a well-defined coastal region. Chapters 2 through 6 describe several locations at which ghostly activity has been reported. Unlike other collections of ghost stories and descriptions of haunted places, this book emphasizes access. Private homes and other buildings not open to visitors are not included. Addresses of each haunted site are provided along with other information to assist you in finding and entering the location. Several appendixes offer organizational material for your ghost hunts, including a Sighting Report Form to document your adventures, lists of suggested reading and videos, Internet resources, and organizations you may contact about your experiences with ghosts.

GHOST HUNTING ON CALIFORNIA'S HAUNTED COAST

The very word *ghost* immediately brings to mind visions of ancient European castles, foggy moors, and dark, wind-swept ramparts where knights battled enemies of the crown or heroines fell to their death. The fact is that ghosts are everywhere. A history based in antiquity and a site that includes dark dungeons, hidden catacombs, or ancient ruins covered with a veil of sorrow and pain is not essential, but contemporary versions of these elements are common in many American cities. On California's central coast, several desolate locations and historic buildings dating from the 18th century have all the ingredients necessary for successful ghost hunting.

California central coast has been inhabited for a thousand years or more by Indians who frequently engaged in intertribal warfare while practicing a spiritual lifestyle that included communication with the dead. Since the late 1770s, the region has also been populated with people from European and Mexican cultures who experienced tremendous changes in their lives. Changes and challenges that were, at times, overwhelming were created by the transition of the region from a wilderness in the 1770s to a Spanish colony and then to a Mexican province in 1820. In less than three decades, Mexico's tenuous hold on the region was broken by relentless Yankee immigration and growing awareness of the untapped economic wealth of the territory. On June 14, 1846, Americans staged the Bear Flag Revolt in Sonoma, which was supported by the arrival of the American fleet under Commodore John Sloat in Monterey Bay. On July 2, 1846, the Stars and Stripes replaced the Mexican flag over the Monterey customs house, fulfilling the American Manifest Destiny.

Just three years later, the calamity of the Gold Rush from 1849 to

1858 brought thousands of people through coastal and valley cities, creating even more turmoil in the region. The growing wealth of cities and towns and the admission of California to the union in 1850 as the 31st state did little to dampen criminal activity, reduce civil disobedience, dissipate racism, or civilize those who abandoned the best qualities of their character while they engaged in the greedy search for gold. Other cataclysmic changes were brought about by armed conflicts, including skirmishes between Indians and white settlers.

Typhoid, diphtheria, smallpox, and cholera epidemics of the late 19th century and the Spanish Flu epidemic of 1918 brought tragedy to many families, ending lives at a young age and filling many pioneer graveyards. In many fascinating burial grounds, such as New Almaden's Hacienda Cemetery, pioneer cemeteries in Pacific Grove and Paso Robles, and the old mission cemeteries in Monterey, San Luis Obispo, and San Miguel, victims are buried in clusters. Some grave markers indicate that entire families comprised of young adults and infants were buried together, creating spirits who have yet to let go and move on.

Catastrophic fires destroyed some coastal towns and settlements in their infancy. Fast-moving blazes destroyed crude wooden shacks and tents, catching many residents off guard and killing them. On April 14, 1894, a fire destroyed downtown Santa Cruz only hours after a water gate at the nearby reservoir had burst, cutting off the water supply. Other towns that suffered from devastating fires include Salinas (1894 and 1906), Santa Cruz (1894), San Lucas (1919), and Paso Robles (1940).

Some of these urban fires also destroyed wooden grave markers in the town cemeteries. During the period of rapid rebuilding that followed these terrible conflagrations, spirits became restless when buildings were constructed over their unmarked graves. In the late 20th and early 21st centuries, construction of parks, homes, businesses, and streets caused desecration of graves, especially those of Native Americans, leading to reports of ghostly activity in modern structures.

As 19th-century gold hunters transitioned from panning gravel in Sierra streams to extracting other valuable minerals from mines in the coastal mountains, considerable wealth was produced but dangers were encountered. Cave-ins, fires, and flooding of mine shafts occurred with alarming frequency, sometimes closing mines that still held vast deposits of mercury, coal, and other valuable materials. In 1859, a mine cave-in at the New Almaden mercury mine, in the Santa Cruz Mountains, killed more than 15 miners. More than a century after the disaster, astonished visitors to the area have reported seeing a large group of men dressed in miner's gear and covered with thick dust emerge form the mine. Ten miles north of New Almaden, near the tiny settlements of Wright's Station and Laurel, a total of 37 Chinese workers lost their lives in explosions on February 12 and November 17, 1879, while they toiled in the darkness digging a railroad tunnel. Gas-triggered explosions caused massive cave-ins, preventing any rescue attempt. Ghosts of these workers still haunt nearby canyons and appear wandering on roads. Groups of three to 10 workers often appear near a train tunnel that is still in use by the Mountain Charlie Railroad of Felton and at the tunnel entrance at Laurel. Several miles south of Monterey, in the Santa Lucia Mountains, another mine disaster took the lives of 70 Chinese coal miners. An explosion triggered a cave-in that was so extensive the mine could not be reopened. Residents of the sparsely populated region report mournful cries of men when the winds blow from the canyon where the mine is located.

Many coastal communities have endured criminal activity and social injustice that have led to hauntings and legends of ghosts. The activities of several 19th-century outlaws produced many used, abused, confused, and forlorn spirits who remained with us after death. The souls of these victims may still seek lost dreams while they remain attached to what little they gained during their difficult lives. The best known of the 19th-century outlaws was Tiburcio Vasquez. Born in Monterey, in 1835, Vasquez killed a man in a barroom fight in 1854 then began a career of murder and theft that ended with his hanging on March 19, 1875. Vasquez left victims in nearly every coastal town, always retiring to his Cantua Creek hideout to evade the lawmen who hunted him.

From 1852 to 1853, the Murrieta gang terrorized towns and ranches from San Luis Obispo to Salinas. These brazen outlaws sometimes sent advance warning to a town to inform the citizens that they planned a visit and any interference would result in the destruction of every building. During the 1850s, gunfights and armed robberies were so common in San Luis Obispo that the decade is still known as the "bloody '50s." Murderers such as Jack Powers, Pio Linares, Nieves Robles, and Jose Antonio Garcia have left enduring legends and victims in unmarked graves throughout the region.

On March 31, 1886, Peter Hemmer and his son, Julius, were hanged from the Pacific Coast Railroad Bridge in Arroyo Grande by an angry mob. This loathsome pair killed their neighbors, Mr. and Mrs. Walker, after a dispute about land boundaries. After their arrest, the Hemmers were jailed for only a few hours before local citizens exacted justice. This event is still commemorated in Arroyo Grande and many believe the ghosts of the criminals haunt the town.

Starting on November 2, 1970, Santa Cruz County endured two and half years of horrendous criminal activity that included 27 murders. The first five victims were Dr. and Mrs. Victor Ohta, their sons Taggart and Derrick, and the doctor's secretary, Dorothy Cadwallader. The conviction of John Linley Frazier and two others responsible for this crime spree did little to quiet the restless spirits of the victims.

Several plane crashes have left ghosts of victims wandering desolate canyons and fields. On February 12, 1935, the U.S.S. *Macon,* a lighter-than-air craft 785 feet long, crashed near Big Sur. Eighty-three people were aboard the airship but only two lost their lives as it plunged into the water near the Big Sur Lighthouse. In 1984, two aircraft collided over San Luis Obispo, killing all 17 people on board. John Denver's fatal crash on October 12, 1997, a short distance offshore from a rocky Pacific Grove beach brought sadness to many people. A small shrine has developed at the crash site, where some people have reported seeing images of Denver and capturing fascinating electronic voice phenomenon they attribute to his ghost. Another famous entertainer, James Dean died September 30, 1955, in a head-on collision near Paso Robles. His ghost has been reported at the crash site at the intersection of Highway 41 and Highway 466.

Historical records dating from the late 18th century indicate hundreds of shipwrecks occurred along the haunted coast. Several ships ran aground and were destroyed by the surf near the Point Pinos Lighthouse in Pacific Grove. In 1875, the *Ventura* sank in the cove at Big Sur and lost half her crew. Train wrecks have also contributed ghosts to the haunted coast. In 1907, 19 people lost their lives when their train derailed a few miles west of Lompoc.

Numerous floods in the Santa Cruz area have resulted in loss of life since the first settlers established homes there. In 1791, the Spanish had to move their newly established mission buildings because they were subject to flooding from the nearby San Lorenzo River. Floods continued throughout the 19th century with major disasters in 1842, 1862, and 1872. In 1955, another historic flood occurred, killing nine people.

The great Loma Prieta earthquake of October 17, 1989, caused extensive damage in every town and city located in Santa Cruz and Monterey Counties. In Santa Cruz, 31 buildings were destroyed, severely injuring 671 and killing six. The destruction was reminiscent of the great San Francisco earthquake of April 18, 1906.

All of these tragic events add to the region's ghost legacy and have left powerful emotional imprints created by the spirits of the dearly departed who felt a need to stay on. A common factor is the loss of life by a sudden, violent event, often at a young age. Unfortunate crew members of the many ships sunk off the treacherous coast, miners, firefighters, airplane passengers, and Indians who died in skirmishes with settlers all passed with great emotional anguish, leaving their souls with an inextinguishable desire to achieve their life's objectives or with a sense of obligation to offer protection to a particular place or person. Some ghosts remain on the earthly plane for revenge or to provide guidance for someone still alive. Many of those who came to California for gold or great wealth from agriculture or land speculation were caught up in their dreams but met with only frustration and failure before dying alone and in poverty. The restless spirits of those who harbored deep resentment, pain, or a desire to complete their unfinished business still roam the towns and back roads of the coastal mountains.

WHAT IS A GHOST?

A ghost is some aspect of the personality, spirit, consciousness, energy, mind, or soul that remains after the body dies. When any of these are detected by the living—through sight, sound, odor, or movement—the manifestation is called an apparition by parapsychologists. The rest of us call it a ghost. How the ghost manifests itself is unknown.

There seems to be a close association, however, between aspects of the entity's life and its manifestation as a ghost. These include a sudden, traumatic death, strong ties to loved ones who survived the entity or to a particular place, unfinished business, strong emotions such as hatred and anger, or a desire for revenge. Some ghosts appear solid and function as living beings because they are unaware they are dead. Others appear as partial apparitions because they are confused about their transition from life to death.

Ghosts differ from other paranormal phenomena by their display of intelligent action. This includes interaction with the living, performance of a purposeful activity, or a response to ongoing changes in the environment. Ghosts may speak to the living to warn of an unforeseen accident or disaster, to give advice, or to express their love, anger, remorse, or disappointment. They may also be trying to complete some project or duty they failed to finish before death. Some ghosts try to move furniture, room decorations, or the like to suit their preferences.

Occasionally, paranormal activity is bizarre, frightening, or dangerous. Witnesses may see objects fly about, hear strange sounds, or experience accidents. This kind of activity is attributed to a poltergeist, or noisy ghost. Most authorities believe that a living person, not the dead, causes these manifestations. Generally, someone under great emotional stress releases psychic energy that creates subtle or spectacular changes in the environment. Noises commonly associated with a poltergeist include tapping on walls or ceilings, heavy footsteps, shattered glass, ringing telephones, and running water. Objects may move about on tables or floors or fly across a room. Furniture may spin or tip over. Dangerous objects such as knives, hammers, or pens may hit people. These poltergeist events may last a few days, a year, or more. Discovery and removal of the emotionally unstable, living person often stops the poltergeist.

HAUNTINGS

Hauntings and ghost apparitions appear similar but they are not the same thing. Many professional ghost hunters and parapsychologists are careful to make a clear distinction between these two kinds of paranormal phenomena. They share a lot of the same features in terms of what witnesses see, feel, or smell, but a haunting may occur without the presence of a spiritual entity or the consciousness of a dead person. People have reported seeing pale, transparent images of the deceased walking in hallways, climbing stairs, sitting in rocking chairs, or sitting on airplanes, trains, buses, and even restaurants. Some have been seen sleeping in beds, hanging by a rope from a tree, or walking through walls. Most commonly, a partial apparition is seen, but witnesses have reported seeing entire armies engaged in battle. Unlike ghosts, hauntings do not display intelligent action with respect to the location—they do not manipulate your new computer—and they do not interact with the living.

Hauntings may be environmental imprints or recordings of something that happened at a location as a result of the repetition of intense emotion. As such, they tend to be associated with a specific place or object, not a particular person. The ghostly figures tend to perform some kind of repetitive task or activity. Sometimes the haunting is so repetitive that witnesses feel as though they are watching a video loop that plays the same brief scene over and over. A good example is the image of a deceased grandmother who makes appearances seated in her favorite rocking chair.

There is a great deal of evidence that people can trigger and experience these environmental recordings by visiting the particular site, touching an object that was a key element of the event, and psychically connecting with the event. Images of hauntings have been picked up on still and video film as well as on digital recordings. The location of strong environmental imprints can also be discovered through devices such as electromagnetic field detectors. Higher magnetic readings have been found at locations where psychics frequently experience hauntings.

HOW DOES A GHOST MANIFEST ITSELF?

Ghosts interact with our environment in a variety of ways that may have something to do with the strength of their personality or the level of confusion concerning their transformation by death. The talents or skills they possessed in life, their personal objectives, or their level of frustration may be their reason for trying to get our attention. Some ghosts create odors or sounds, particularly those associated with their habits, such as cigar smoke or whistling. Many reports mention the odors of tobacco, oranges, and hemp as most common. Sounds, including voice messages, may be detected with an audio recorder (see Electronic Audio Phenomena). Ghost hunters have recorded greetings, warnings, screams, sobbing, and expressions of love.

One of the most common ghostly activities is moving objects. Ghosts like to knock over stacks of cards or coins, turn doorknobs, scatter matchsticks, and move your keys. For many, it appears easy to manipulate light switches and TV remotes, move windows or doors, or push chairs around. Some ghosts have the power to throw objects, pull pictures from a wall, or move heavy items. As a rule, ghosts cannot tolerate disturbances within the place they haunt. If you tilt a wall-mounted picture, the ghost will set it straight. Obstacles placed in the ghost's path may be pushed aside. These seemingly minor indications of ghostly activity should be recorded for future reference on the Sighting Report Form in Appendix A.

Ghosts can also create changes in the physical qualities of an environment. Ice-cold breezes and unexplained gusts of wind are often the first signs that a ghost is present. Moving or stationary cold spots with temperatures several degrees below surrounding areas have been detected with reliable instruments. Temperature changes sometimes occur with a feeling that the atmosphere has thickened as if the room were suddenly filled with unseen people.

In searching for ghosts, some people use devices that detect changes in magnetic, electrical, or radio fields. However, detected changes may be subject to error, interference by other electrical devices, or misinterpretation. Measurements indicating the presence of a ghost may be difficult to capture on a permanent record.

Ghosts may create images such as luminous fogs, balls of light called orbs, streaks of light, or the partial outline of body parts on still cameras (film or digital) and video recorders. In the 1860s, this was called spirit photography. Modern digital photographs are easily edited and make it difficult to produce convincing proof of ghostly activity.

Humanoid images are the prized objective of most ghost hunters but they are the least experienced. When such images occur, they are often partial, revealing only a head and torso with an arm or two. Feet are seldom seen. Full body apparitions are extremely rare. Some ghost hunters have seen ethereal, fully transparent forms that are barely discernible. Others report seeing ghosts who appear as solid as a living being.

WHY DO GHOSTS REMAIN AT A PARTICULAR PLACE?

Ghosts remain in a particular place because they are emotionally attached to a room, a building, or special surroundings that profoundly affected them during their lives or to activities or events that played a role in their death. A prime example is the haunted house inhabited by the ghost of a man who hanged himself in the master bedroom because his wife left him. It is widely believed that death and sudden transition from the physical world confuse a ghost. He or she remains in familiar or emotionally stabilizing surroundings to ease the strain. A place-bound ghost is most likely to occur when a violent death occurred with great emotional anguish. Ghosts may linger in a house, barn, cemetery, factory, or store waiting for a loved one or anyone familiar that might help them deal with their new level of existence. Some ghosts wander through buildings or forests, on bridges, or alongside particular sections of roads. Some await enemies, seeking revenge. Others await a friend for a chance to resolve their guilt.

UNDER WHAT CONDITIONS IS A SIGHTING MOST LIKELY?

Although ghosts may appear at any time, a sighting may occur on special holidays, anniversaries, birthdays, or during historic periods (July 4, December 7), or calendar periods pertaining to the personal history of the ghost. Halloween is reputed to be a favorite night for many apparitions, while others seem to prefer their own special day or night, on a weekly or monthly cycle.

Night is a traditional time for ghost activity, yet experienced ghost hunters know that sightings may occur at any time. There seems to be no consistent affinity of ghosts for darkness, but they seldom appear when artificial light is bright. Perhaps this is why ghosts shy away from camera crews and their array of lights. Ghosts seem to prefer peace and quiet although some of them have been reported to make incessant, loud sounds. Even a small group of ghost hunters may make too much noise to facilitate a sighting. For this reason, it is recommended that you limit your group to four persons and oral communication be kept to a minimum.

IS GHOST HUNTING DANGEROUS?

Ghost hunting can be hazardous, but reports of injuries inflicted by ghosts are rare and their veracity suspect. Movies and children's ghost stories have created a widespread notion that ghosts may harm the living or even cause the death of persons they dislike. In 2006, a popular television program showed a fascinating video of a ghost hunter being struck down by his camera equipment. The man's heavy equipment moved suddenly from a position at his waist and struck him on the side of the face. Video of this event was interpreted as evidence of a ghost attack but no apparition or light anomaly was visible. Decades ago, the Abbot of Trondheim ghost was reputed to have attacked some people, but circumstances and precipitating events are unclear.

Many authorities believe that rare attacks by ghosts are a matter of mistaken identity, i.e., the ghost misidentified a living person as a figure the ghost knew during his life. It is possible that encounters that appear to be attacks may be nothing more than clumsy efforts by a ghost to achieve recognition. Witnesses of ghost appearances have found themselves in the middle of gunfights, major military battles, and other violent events yet sustained not the slightest injury.

Persons who claim to have been injured by a ghost have, in most cases, precipitated the injury themselves through their own ignorance or fear. Ghost hunters often carry out investigations in the dark or subdued light and may encounter environmental hazards that lead to injury. Fear may trigger an attempt to race from a haunted site, exposing the ghost hunter to injury by tripping over unseen objects or making contact with broken glass, low-hanging tree limbs, exposed wiring, or weakened floorboards, stairways, or doorways.

The ghost hunter will be safe if he keeps a wary eye and a calm attitude and sets aside tendencies to fear the ghost or the circumstances of its appearance. Safety may be enhanced if you visit a haunted location while it is well illuminated, during daylight hours for instance. Potential hazards in the environment can be identified and, perhaps, cleared or marked with light-reflecting tape.

Most authorities agree that ghosts do not travel. Ghosts will not follow you home, take up residence in your car, or attempt to occupy your body. They are held in a time and space by deep emotional ties to an event or place. Ghosts have been observed on airplanes, trains, buses, and ships; however, it is unlikely that the destination interests them. Something about the journey, some event such as a plane crash or train wreck, accounts for their appearance as travelers. In some cases, it is the conveyance that ties the ghost to the physical plane. A vintage World War II B-17 bomber may be haunted by the ghost of a man who piloted that type of aircraft in the 1940s. A ship, such as the *Queen Mary* in Long Beach may be an irresistible attraction for the ghost of a sailor who once worked on passenger liners.

HOT SPOTS FOR GHOSTLY ACTIVITY

Numerous sites of disasters, criminal activity, suicides, devastating fires, and other tragic events abound on California's haunted coast, providing hundreds of opportunities for ghost hunting. You may visit the locations described in Chapters 2 through 6 to experience ghostly activity discovered by others or discover a hot spot to research and initiate your own ghost investigation.

Astute ghost hunters often search historical maps, drawings, and other documents to find the sites of military conflicts, buildings that no longer exist, or sites of tragic events now occupied by modern structures. For example, maps and drawings found online or displayed in museums such as the Presidio of Monterey, Boronda Adobe History Center in Salinas, and the Monterey History and Maritime Museum or historic locations such as San Juan Bautista State Historic Park may be a good place to start.

People who died in mine disasters or train or stagecoach robberies, of epidemics, or from infections that ensued after minor injuries and those displaced by other tragic events such as fires may haunt the site of their graves, favorite bars or restaurants, workplaces, or cherished homes. In historic neighborhoods of some of the larger coastal cities, homes of many well-known residents are often the focal point for ghost investigations. Among the most famous historic homes are those of American consul Thomas Oliver Larkin and Robert Louis Stevenson in Monterey, Lt. Gov. William Jeter in Santa Cruz, Chinese merchant Ah Louis and grape grower Pierre Hyppolite Dallidet in San Luis Obispo, Mexican general Jose Castro in San Juan Bautista, and the world-famous Hearst Castle at San Simeon.

Fascinating histories and ghostly atmospheres may also be found in historic homes that are now modern businesses, such as Stokes Restaurant, housed in the vintage 1833 Stokes adobe, and the Casa Munras Hotel, part of an 1825 hacienda, both in Monterey. In Carmel, the legendary La Playa Hotel occupies the former home of Christopher Jorgensen and Angela Ghirardelli, heiress of the San Francisco chocolate fortune. The haunted Brothers' Restaurant in Los Olivos occupies Mattei's Tavern, a former stagecoach inn for travelers between Los Angeles and San Francisco.

Some towns have established historic districts and other venues that have been investigated by professional and amateur ghost hunters. These include the preserved and restored structures of San Luis Obispo, the historic plaza of San Juan Bautista, Cannery Row in Monterey, the New Almaden Mine near San Jose, and the many buildings that comprise the Monterey State Historic Park. Some of the best places for ghost hunting include Doc Ricketts' lab on Monterey's Cannery Row, John Steinbeck's house in Salinas, the Zanetta House in San Juan Bautista, the Hinds Victorian Guest House in Santa Cruz, and Brookdale Lodge in Felton.

California's historic Spanish missions, spanning 500 miles from San Diego to Sonoma, offer ghost hunters many opportunities to discover paranormal activity generated by Indians, mission priests, Spanish and Mexican soldiers, Yankee settlers, and veterans of the Civil War. Built of adobe bricks and stone, most of the 21 missions, separated by one day's travel on horseback, are restored and open to the public. Some of the missions of the haunted coast are within view of the ocean, while others are a short distance inland. They include Santa Cruz, San Carlos de Borromeo in Carmel, San Juan Bautista, Nuestra Senora de la Soledad, San Antonio de Paduan near San Lucas, San Miguel Arcangel, San Luis Obispo de Tolosa, La Purisima Concepcion in Lompoc, and Santa Inez in Solvang. Each one has a cemetery but several hundred unmarked graves lay under walks and parking areas. At each mission, subjugation of the local Indians, usually with harsh treatment, ultimately destroyed the local native culture. Epidemics, droughts, famine, and occasional skirmishes with Spanish soldiers led to early death and the demise of local tribes. Restless spirits of Native Americans are often encountered on mission grounds, together with the ghosts of priests, Spanish and Mexican soldiers, and 19th-century travelers who sought sanctuary after an arduous journey across country from the distant U.S.

Many churches established in the 19th and early 20th centuries exist throughout the haunted coast region and are still surrounded by graveyards that contain pioneers and notable historic figures. Built in a Gothic style, the First Presbyterian Church of San Luis Obispo was dedicated in 1905. The church replaced a wooden structure that was built in 1878. Farther north, the Estrella Church of Paso Robles (1879), the Presbyterian Church of San Martin (1904), the Christian Church of Gilroy (1870), and the Calvary Episcopalian Church of Santa Cruz (1864) are restored and accessible to the general public as places of historical interest while they continue to offer worship services.

Founded on June 3, 1770, the Royal Presidio Chapel in Monterey stands as one of the oldest places of worship in the western United States. It was designated as a "royal" church because California's Spanish governor worshiped there in his role as representative of the king of Spain. Built by local Indians under the direction of Manuel Ruiz, its ornate Spanish period architectural features, musty veil of history, and ghostly atmosphere make this a popular destination for ghost hunters.

Several cemeteries are scattered about the coast and are known by local ghost hunters as good places to experience paranormal phenomena. Many of them date from the late 18th century with fascinating architecture, epitaphs, and overgrown foliage, all of which combine to create a spooky atmosphere. These cities of the dead include some unusual tombs and crypts, some marked by peculiar monuments, and unmarked mass graves.

The Skylawn Cemetery on Highway 92, near Half Moon Bay, was opened in the 1930s to serve a wild and thriving community of loggers, fishermen, ranchers, and saloon owners. Hundreds of people who have driven by the cemetery at night have noticed a woman sitting in the back seat of their car. Dressed in 1970s-style clothing, the woman remains silent but smiles as if she is pleased to have found a ride home from the scene of her fatal accident on Highway 92. Other spirits in this spooky cemetery create orbs in photographs and digital images or create cold spots and that creepy feeling that the visitor is being watched or touched by invisible hands.

A few miles from downtown Santa Cruz, the Graham Hill Road Cemetery houses the remains of locals who served as Union soldiers, sailors, and marines during the Civil War. This cemetery opened in 1862, in time to offer a final resting place to loggers and train operators who died in the many disasters that occurred in the forests of the Santa Cruz Mountains.

Miners who lost their lives in the New Almaden mercury mines were interred in the Hacienda Cemetery near San Jose. Surrounded by historic buildings that comprise Almaden Quicksilver County Park, the place is known for intense paranormal activity due, perhaps, to the tragic, early death that befell many of its occupants. The oddest grave in the cemetery is that of the arm of Bertram Barrett. As a teenager in 1898, Barrett lost his arm in an accident. When he died in 1959, the remainer of his body was buried in San Jose's Oak Hill Cemetery.

On the Monterey peninsula, several cemeteries keep ghost hunters busy. The San Carlos Cemetery, established in 1834, spreads over 13.5 acres and contains more than a thousand crypts. Spanish soldiers, members of the Mexican militia, and many founding members of Monterey are buried here. Nearby, the Cemeterio El Encinal (Cemetery of Many Oaks) has been the target of ghost hunters who seek the spirits of famous people buried here, including a local character known as

"She was always right" Emma Johnsons (1844-1884); Flora Woods-Adams (1876-1948), the outrageous madam of John Steinbeck's *Cannery Row;* and another real-life Steinbeck character, Edward "Doc" Ricketts (1897-1948).

In Carmel, the cemetery of the Mission San Carlos Borromeo de Carmelo has a small cemetery but the number of bodies buried there may exceed 3,000. Weathered tombstones and wooden markers decorate the graves of priests and church officials, but it is known that thousands of Indians and destitute Mexicans and Americans were buried on mission grounds after epidemics swept through the area. Other mission cemeteries, particularly those at Mission San Juan Bautista, Mission Nuestra Senora de la Soledad near Soledad, Mission San Miguel, and Mission San Antonio de Padua near King City, are spiritually active, giving ghost hunters opportunities to experience the paranormal.

The most fascinating and spiritually active cemetery in the coast region is Adelaida Cemetery near Paso Robles. Opened in 1859, the cemetery is filled with people who died from epidemics and mercury poisoning from mines that supported the Adelaida community. The ghost of Charlotte Sitton fascinates local ghost hunters who have nicknamed her the Pink Lady for the flowing pink gown she wears as she lays flowers on the graves of her children.

Most county Web sites list pioneer cemeteries and offer links to local organizations that care for the graves and grounds. The best way to see the cemeteries of the haunted coast and learn fascinating histories of those entombed is to tour them with a knowledgeable guide. (See Appendix F: Tours and Events.) Some of these places are too spooky and possibly unsafe after dark unless you are accompanied by people who can insure a pleasant visit.

LOCAL GHOST HUNTERS

Several local organizations conduct investigations into ghostly activity and other paranormal phenomena in California's central coast region. They can help you locate haunted sites, provide information about previous ghost investigations they have conducted, or sharpen your skills as a paranormal investigator. These organizations include San Francisco Ghost Society, Haunted and Paranormal Investigations (HPI), Central Coast Paranormal Investigators, Ghost Trackers, the San Gabriel Valley Ghost Hunters Society, the California Society for Ghost Research, and Ventura Haunts. The activities of these organizations have been featured in a variety of news media. Their investigators combine advanced high-tech approaches to ghost hunting with the insight of psychics to produce some amazing results. HPI and Ghost Trackers also host special events and offer classes and training seminars. See Appendix E (Internet Resources) for contact information. Tours of haunted places are available in Monterey and Ventura (see Appendix F). If you inquire at a local bookshop or historical society, you may meet a history buff or ghost hunter who can take you places tourists never hear about.

TWO SIMPLE RULES

Two simple rules apply for successful ghost hunting. The first is to be patient. Ghosts are everywhere, but contact may require a considerable investment of time. The second rule is to have fun. You may report your ghost-hunting experiences or suggest hot spots for ghost hunting to the author via e-mail at ghosthunter@jeffdwyer.com. Visit the author's Web site at www.jeffdwyer.com.

Ghost Hunter's Guide
to
Monterey and
California's Central
Coast

CHAPTER 1

How to Hunt Ghosts

You may want to visit recognized haunted sites, listed in Chapters 2 through 6, using some of the ghost-hunting techniques described later in this chapter or search for a new haunted site. If you are looking for a haunted place that has not yet been discovered, start with an old house in your neighborhood or a favorite historic bed-and-breakfast inn. You may get a lead from fascinating stories about ancestors that have been passed down through your family, rumors circulating among your friends and neighbors, or reports posted on the Internet.

Your search for a ghost or exploration of a haunted place starts with research. Summaries of obscure and esoteric material about possible haunted sites are available from museums, local historical societies, and bookstores. Brochures and booklets, sold at historical sites under the California State Parks system, can be good resources too.

Guided tours of historical sites such as the preserved 19th-century buildings in old Monterey; old neighborhoods in towns such as San Luis Obispo, Morro Bay, Salinas, and Santa Cruz; the historic plaza of San Juan Bautista; or old churches and missions, mines, and pioneer cemeteries throughout the coastal mountains are good places to begin your research. Tours can help you develop a feel for places within a building where ghosts might be sighted or an appreciation of relevant history. Ghost, cemetery, and history tours of fascinating towns on the California coast are popular and offer a good way to learn a lot about local paranormal activity in a short time.

By touring haunted buildings, you will have opportunities to speak with guides and docents who may be able to provide you with clues about the dearly departed or tell you ghost stories you can't find in published material. Docents may know people—old-timers in the area or amateur historians—who can give you additional information about a site, its former owners or residents, and its potential for ghostly activity.

Almost every city has a local historical society (see Appendix G). These are good places to find information that may not be published anywhere else. This could be histories of local families and buildings; information about tragedies, disasters, criminal activity, or legends; and myths about places that may be haunted. You will want to take notes about secret scandals or other ghost-producing happenings that occurred at locations now occupied by modern buildings, roads, or parks. In these cases, someone occupying a new house or other structure could hear strange sounds, feel cold spots, or see ghosts or spirit remnants.

Newspapers are an excellent source of historical information as well. You can search for articles about ghosts, haunted places, or paranormal activity by accessing the newspaper's archives via the Internet and entering key words, dates, or names. Newspaper articles about suicides, murders, train wrecks, plane crashes, and suspected or documented paranormal phenomena can provide essential information for your ghost hunt. Stories about authentic haunted sites are common around Halloween.

Bookstores and libraries usually have special-interest sections with books on local history by local writers. A few inquiries may connect you with these local writers, who may be able to help you focus your research.

If these living souls cannot help, try the dead. A visit to a local graveyard is often useful in identifying possible ghosts. Often you can find headstones that indicate the person entombed died of suicide, criminal activity, local disaster, or such. Some epitaphs may indicate if the deceased was survived by a spouse and children or died far from home. Grave markers that have been desecrated or damaged by weather, vegetation, erosion, or earthquakes are good places to look for paranormal phenomena.

Perhaps the best place to start a search for a ghost is within your own family. Oral histories can spark your interest in a particular ancestor, scandal, building, or site relevant to your family. Old photographs, death certificates, letters and wills, anniversary lists in family Bibles, and keepsakes can be great clues. Then you can visit gravesites or homes of your ancestors to check out the vibes as you mentally and emotionally empathize with specific aspects of your family's history.

Almost every family has a departed member who died at an early age, suffered hardships or emotional anguish, or passed away suddenly due to an accident or natural disaster. Once you have focused your research on a deceased person, you need to determine if that person remains on this earthly plane as a ghost. Evaluate the individual's personal history to see if he had a reason to remain attached to a specific place.

Was his death violent or occur under tragic circumstances?

Did he die at a young age with unfinished business?

Did the deceased leave behind loved ones who needed his support and protection?

Was this person attached to a specific site or building?

Would the individual be inclined to seek revenge against those responsible for his death?

Would his devotion and sense of loyalty lead him to offer eternal companionship to loved ones?

Revenge, anger, refusal to recognize the reality of transformation by death, and other negative factors prompt many spirits to haunt places and people. However, most ghosts are motivated by positive factors. Spirits may remain at a site to offer protection to a loved one or a particular place.

Also, remember that ghosts can appear as animals or objects. Apparitions of ships, buildings, covered wagons, bridges, and roads by the strictest definitions are phantoms. A phantom is the essence of a structure that no longer exists on the physical plane. Many people have seen houses, cottages, castles, villages and large ships that were destroyed or sunk years before.

BASIC PREPARATION FOR GHOST HUNTING

If you decide to ghost hunt at night or on a special anniversary, make a trip to the site a few days ahead of time. During daylight hours, familiarize yourself with the place and its surroundings. Many historical sites are closed after sunset or crowded at certain times by organized tours.

TWO BASIC METHODS FOR FINDING GHOSTS

Based partly on the kind of paranormal activity reported at a site, the ghost hunter must decide which method or approach will be used. Some will feel competent with a collection of cameras, electromagnetic field detectors, digital thermometers, computers, data recorders, and other high-tech gadgets. These ghost hunters prefer to use the Technical Approach. Others may discover they have an emotional affinity for a particular historic site, a surprising fascination with an event associated with a haunting, or empathy for a deceased person. These ghost hunters may have success with the Psychic Approach. Another consideration is the ghost hunter's goal. Some desire scientific evidence of ghostly presence while others simply want to experience paranormal activity.

THE TECHNICAL APPROACH

Professional and advanced amateur ghost hunters often use an array of detection and recording devices that cover a wide range of the electromagnetic spectrum. This approach can be complicated, expensive, and require technically skilled people to operate the devices. Ghost hunters who want to keep their investigations simple get satisfying results with common audio and video recording devices and other low-tech methods.

Equipment Preparation

A few days before your ghost hunt, purchase fresh film for your camera and tape for audio recording devices or clear the media of previous recordings. Test your batteries and bring new backup batteries and freshly charged power packs to the investigation site. You should have two types of flashlights: a broad-beam light for moving around a site and a penlight-type flashlight for narrow-field illumination while you make notes or adjust equipment. A red lens will help you avoid disruption of your night-adapted vision. A candle is a good way to light the site in a way that is least offensive to a ghost.

Still-Photography Techniques

Many photographic techniques that work well under normal conditions are inadequate for ghost hunts. That's because ghost hunting is usually conducted under conditions of low ambient light. This requires the use of long exposures. Some investigators use a strobe or flash device but these can make the photos look unauthentic or create artifacts.

If you use film-based photography, practice taking photos with films of various light sensitivities before you go on your ghost hunt. Standard photographic films of high light sensitivity should be used—ASA of 800 or higher is recommended. At a dark or nearly dark location, mount the camera on a tripod. Try several exposure settings, from one to 30 seconds, and aperture settings under various low-light conditions. Your equipment should include a stable, light-weight tripod. Hand-held cameras may produce poorly focused photographs when the exposure duration is greater that $\frac{1}{60}$ second

Make notes about the camera settings that work best under various light conditions. Avoid aiming the camera at a scene where there is a bright light such as a street lamp or exit sign over a doorway. These light sources may "overflow" throughout your photograph.

Some professional and advanced amateur ghost hunters use infrared film. You should consult a professional photo lab technician about this type of film and its associated photographic techniques. Infrared photography can yield some amazing pictures of spirits not detected by other means. It has been theorized that spiritual entities exist at a frequency that lies below that of the visual spectrum of humans. By using a camera filter that blocks out visible light while admitting infrared light, images of ghosts may be obtained. Infrared film has become scarce and expensive since 2007, when manufacturers such as Kodak encountered a significant decline in the demand for the product. However, digital cameras are inherently sensitive to infrared light, and minor adjustments allow users to take pictures that may reveal entities that would not be seen with conventional photographic techniques. In some digital cameras, these adjustments are quite easy, requiring nothing more than selecting a "night vision" mode.

Ghost hunters have also employed Polaroid-type cameras with interesting results. The rapid film-developing system used by these cameras gives almost instant feedback about your technique and/ or success in documenting ghost activities. Ghosts have reportedly written messages on Polaroid film.

If you use digital photographic methods, practice taking pictures under conditions of low ambient light, with and without artificial lighting. Most digital cameras have default automatic settings that might not well work during a ghost investigation. These settings may not be easily changed as ambient conditions change at the haunted site unless you have practiced the procedures. Many cameras have features that enable automatic exposures at specific intervals, e.g., once every minute. This allows a hands-off remote photograph record to be made. Repetitive automatic exposures also allow a site to be investigated without the presence of the investigator.

While every ghost hunter armed with a camera wishes to capture the full-bodied image of a ghost, most have to settle for light anomalies. These may be amorphous, luminescent clouds or narrow streaks of light resembling a shooting star. The light anomaly most frequently captured on film and in digital images is the orb. An orb is a symmetrical white disk that appears most often in photographs and digital images made under low-light conditions. It may appear hovering near a ceiling, over a bed, or inside a car. A photograph may contain a single orb or show so many of varying sizes that they cannot be counted. Impressive pictures of light anomalies may be viewed at several Web sites.

Many ghost hunters claim that orbs are spirit manifestations without explaining why the spirit of a human would appear as a disk of light. Some of these have a humanoid shape but fail to convince critics and skeptics that the image is that of a ghost because the image is so perfectly illuminated it appears fake. Software for processing digital images has reduced the power of proof that was once attributed to photographs. Critics and skeptics also point out that orbs may be the result of bugs, dust particles, or water droplets suspended in the air close to the lens or inside the camera. Excited ghost hunters have displayed pictures of light anomalies that turn out to be the result of wisps of hair, a camera strap, a finger, cigarette smoke, light reflected from jewelry, or smudges on the lens.

It is interesting to note that orbs were virtually unheard-of in the field of paranormal investigation until digital cameras became available. Consequently, many people suspect that orbs may be the result of the camera's operating characteristics. Under conditions of low light, digital pixels may not fill in completely. This has been called under-pixelation. As a result, no image information or electronic signal is generated. The lack of a signal is detected by the camera's software, which then fills in the missing spot in the picture's signal array with white light. The result is an orb.

Is it possible that a spirit will manifest as an orb? Yes, although many experts suggest that as many as 99 percent of orb pictures do not represent anything paranormal. I've seen some very impressive orbs, however. Ghost hunter Jackie Ganiy, president of Sonoma SPIRIT, captured a picture of an orb hovering over the flight deck of the aircraft carrier USS *Hornet* in Alameda, California. This orb was symmetrically rounded but a skull was visible within it. Books by Melvyn Willin and Troy Taylor present fascinating collections of the best pictures of ghosts and other paranormal light anomalies, including orbs.

Generally, light anomalies alone should not be readily accepted as evidence of a spirit. They should be captured along with audio phenomena, changes in electromagnetic field, isolated changes in air temperature, or other still or video images. Evidence might also be found in psychic impressions experienced at the time and place that the light anomaly was captured. Psychic impressions of intense emotions, sobbing, cries for help, or screaming might be obtained while standing in an old hospital room as a photographer captures a picture of an orb hovering over the bed.

Audio Recording Techniques

Tape or digital recorders provide an inexpensive way to obtain audio evidence of ghostly activity. The popular term for this is electronic voice phenomena or EVP. The American Association for EVP defines the phenomena as any intelligible voice detected on recording media that has no known explanation. Most ghost hunters accept a wider definition that includes the sound of moving objects such as doors, windows, or glass objects; whistling; sobbing; laughter; screams; humming; gunshots; footsteps; explosions; musical notes; or tapping and knocking. Given this wide variety of sounds, I have proposed that the term EVP be replaced by EAP, electronic audio phenomena, and defined as any audio recording that cannot be attributed to normal phenomena.

EAP are obtained as a ghost hunter operates an audio recording device while investigating an allegedly haunted place. The ghost hunter may record EAP while remaining stationary at a site, such as next to a grave, or while walking around a location. This is called an EAP or EVP sweep. Generally, questions are asked to which spirits may respond. These questions should be simple and follow an invitation for any spirits present to communicate, even if only by sound. Typical questions include:

What is your name?

Did you die here?

How old are you?

Do you want me to leave?

Why are you here?

Your research may indicate specific questions you can use in your EAP investigations. If you seek a ghost of a farm worker who committed suicide by hanging himself in a barn, you may ask, "Did you die in this barn?" and "Did you hang yourself?" The ghost hunter may also provoke a spirit through verbal confrontation or insult.

In most cases, spirit responses cannot be heard by the ghost hunter but they may be discovered on the audio recording during playback. Typically, responses are brief, rarely lasting more than a few seconds. Vocalizations sometimes have amazing clarity but most often they are unintelligible and, as with other sounds, rarely repeated in subsequent recordings. If the spirit's response comprises a clear and reasonable answer to the question, the recording may be called a "specific" EAP. Other responses, whether they are vocalizations or other sounds, must be labeled "random" EAP and scrutinized as the result of processes that are not paranormal. For example, the sound of a conversation between two living people may be carried a long distance across a body of water. A ghost hunter who is unaware of others in the area may ask, "What is your name?" The response discovered during playback may be "I am cold." This is a random EAP and likely a non-paranormal recording of words spoken by a living person. Random EAP may also be created by natural or normal processes such as the wind against a window or drafts in an old house, and there is high likelihood that they do not reflect a spirit's intelligent interaction with the investigator. Specific EAP has greater value as evidence of a ghostly presence because clear and reasonable responses to specific questions are not likely to be created by the random conversations of living people nearby or by natural processes.

Often, EAP consists of nonvocal sounds. Musical instruments, slamming doors, gunshots, footsteps, and tapping sounds may be evoked by the ghost hunter's questions. Ghosts that are unable to generate vocalizations may resort to these sounds as the only means of communication. These may be random EAP but still comprise good evidence of a ghostly presence. You may ask, "Why are you here?" On playback, the recording may reveal the sound of footsteps moving away from the microphone. In this instance, the ghost may have been troubled by the question and decided to leave.

While EAP are seldom heard through the human auditory sense, they may be captured on recording media by one of two ways. Spirits may encode their intention or effort to create sound telepathically onto the magnetic tape or electronics of the recording device by manipulation of its internal electromagnetic fields. Another theory holds that a vocalization, musical note, or other sound that was previously imprinted on the electromagnetic field of the environment may be triggered to "play" by the ghost hunter and detected by the recording device. In the case of the latter, the EAP is typically random, suggesting no spirit is present, but the experience is still paranormal. Ghost hunters who have exceptional luck in acquiring paranormal audio recordings have been called EVP magnets.

Before you begin your EAP sweep, test your recorder under conditions you expect to find at the investigation site in order to reduce audio artifacts and ensure optimal performance of the device. Does your recorder pick up excessive background noise? This may obscure ghostly sounds. If so, consider upgrading the tape quality or select a high-quality digital audio recorder. Also, consider using a wind guard on the microphone.

Consider using two or more recorders at different locations within the site. This allows you to verify sounds such as wind against a window and reduce the possibility of ambiguous recordings or misinterpretation of an EAP.

Allow time, between 15 and 60 seconds, for a response. EAP can be heard only during playback, so ghost hunters should review recordings every 5 to 10 minutes during the investigation, rather than waiting until the investigation is completed. This will enable the identification of hot spots for spirit activity that may be investigated more thoroughly.

You can use sound-activated recorders at a site overnight. They will automatically switch on whenever a sound occurs above a minimum threshold. Be aware that tape recorders may yield recordings that start with an annoying artifact, the result of a slow tape speed, at the beginning of each recorded segment. The slow tape speed could obscure the sounds made by a ghost.

Remote microphones and monitor earphones allow you to remain some distance from the site and activate the recorder when ghostly sounds are heard. If this equipment is not available, use long-play modes (60-90 minutes or more), turn the recorder on, and let it run throughout your investigation, whether you remain stationary or walk about the site.

Wear a lapel microphone connected to a small audio recorder carried in your pocket. Operated in the sound-activation mode, this device will also provide you with a means of making audio notes rather than written notes. A headset with a microphone is especially useful with this technique.

Ghost hunters must carefully analyze their audio recordings and the environment in which they are obtained to be certain they are not inadvertent recordings of natural or normal sounds. Sound may carry great distances, particularly over bodies of water and when there is fog or low cloud cover. If a tape recorder is used, a new tape may reduce the chances of artifact. I recommend computer software such as Adobe Audition for editing your EAP recording. With a little practice, you will be able to subdue or eliminate extraneous sounds while enhancing spirit communications.

The American Association for EVP maintains a Web site for general information and advice: www.AA-EVP.com. Several Web sites may be accessed to hear examples of EVP. Use the keyword search "EVP" to locate them.

Video Recording

Video recorders offer a wide variety of recording features from time-lapse to auto-start/stop and autofocus. These features enable you to make surveillance-type recordings over many hours while you are off-site. Consult your user's manual for low-light recording guidelines and always use a tripod and long-duration battery packs.

If you plan to attempt video recording, consider using two recorders set at equal distance from a specific object such as a chair. Arrange the recorders at different angles, preferably 90 degrees from each other.

Another approach you might try is to use a wide-angle setting on the first camera for a broad view of a room, porch, or courtyard. On the second camera, use a closeup setting to capture ghostly apparitions at a door, chair, or window.

You may have more success with sequential, manual, or timer-actuated recordings than a continuous-run technique. If you try this technique, use recording runs of one to five minutes. Practice using the method that interrupts the automatic setting should you need to manually control the recording process. Always use a tripod that can be moved to a new location in a hurry.

High-Tech Equipment

You can buy devices such as electromagnetic field detectors, infrared thermometers, barometers, and motion detectors at your local electronics store or over the Internet. Good online sources for high-tech ghost hunting equipment are the Society for Paranormal Investigation, the Ghost Hunter Store, and the EMF Safety Superstore.

Inexpensive, battery-operated motion detectors can be placed at several locations within an investigation site. Some of these allow users to select an audio signal or a silent flashing light signal and connect the output to a central monitor. These devices work by measuring optical or acoustical changes in the environment. Therefore, they are most reliable when remote surveillance is performed and investigators are certain that no living beings have entered the site.

Infrared thermometers have been used to search for cold spots that may signal the presence of a ghost. While these devices are widely utilized and sometimes displayed on paranormal TV shows, they are often used incorrectly. They cannot assess changes in the temperature of clear air because of its very low density and minimal emission of infrared energy. However, infrared thermometers can detect the surface temperature of solid objects, liquids, dense gases, and clouds. With a laser to assist aiming, the device can be used to measure the temperature of objects that cannot be reached due to obstructions such as fences and hazards such as bodies of water that cannot be crossed, unsafe structures, or animals.

Night vision goggles can be useful in low-light situations. These devices enhance the intensity of light within the visual spectrum and augment the resulting image with nonvisual sources of electromagnetic radiation such as near-infrared or ultraviolet light. Night vision devices enable users to see doors and other objects move that otherwise might be difficult to see. The resulting scene appears monochromatic but preserves fine details.

The most advanced and expensive piece of equipment used by ghost hunters is the FLIR imaging device. This acronym stands for forward-looking infrared. FLIRs detect thermal energy in the infrared range. The FLIR lens focuses the scene on a vast array of sensors that produce thousands of simultaneous measurements of thermal energy. Software then assembles the thermal measurements into a mosaic or picture that is displayed on a hand-held video screen. In the picture, elements of the scene are colored according to the temperature or level of infrared radiation. The result resembles a coloring-book image in which some elements are blue, indicating colder temperatures, while others are yellow, orange, or red, indicating warmer temperatures.

FLIR systems can see through atmospheric obscurants such as smoke or fog and in total darkness. Ghost hunters use them to detect spirits that do not generate an image within the human visual spectrum. Theoretically, when spirits appear on our plane they draw energy from the environment, creating a cold spot. A FLIR will detect subtle changes in temperature and depict the shape of the cold spot on the video screen. When the shape of the cold spot is humanoid, ghost hunters claim they have evidence that a ghost is present.

Despite the technical sophistication and expense of FLIRs, the images they produce may be misinterpreted. FLIRs may detect sources of heat or cold created by normal processes not noticed by the user. A living being who occupied the scene moments before a FLIR-equipped ghost hunter arrived may leave residual heat in a chair or on a doorknob. Finding the scene unoccupied by any living being, the ghost hunter might mistakenly cite the detected thermal anomaly as evidence of a ghostly presence.

Electromagnetic field (EMF) detectors are used by paranormal investigators to detect the presence of ghosts in spite of the lack of scientific evidence that EMF and spirit presence are linked. Ghost hunters who use EMF detectors claim that spikes in a local electromagnetic field are created when a ghost transitions onto our plane of existence. These devices, however, often pick up EMF generated by unseen electrical appliances, faulty wiring in an old house, cell phones, walkie-talkies, video recorders, and numerous other sources, including solar flares and geomagnetic storms. EMF detectors may be useful if proper controls are established and all possible sources of natural EMF are identified.

Electronic gadgets can be useful and fun, but unless you have a means of creating a record of the instrument's output or storing images or data in a computer, your reports of light anomalies, apparent paranormal motion of objects, changes in the physical characteristics of the environment, or apparitions will not constitute the kind of hard evidence you need to satisfy skeptics. Keep in mind that even expensive instruments may produce erroneous data or signals if they are incorrectly calibrated, misused, or improperly maintained. Also, data can be easily misinterpreted if the user does not understand the technical or operating limitations of the device. Using expensive high-tech gadgets does not guarantee accurate results, nor do they validate a ghost hunt as a scientific investigation.

Low-Tech Methods

I have had great success in detecting spirit activity with common household items. Ghosts often become active when they are irritated by changes in their favored environment. If you tilt a picture hanging on the wall, leave an object in the ghost's rocking chair, or leave a book open, a ghost may straighten the picture, remove the object from his chair, or close the book.

Spirits may be attracted to objects they can manipulate easily. Leave four aces at the top of a deck of cards. A ghost may shuffle them throughout the deck. Ghosts are often attracted to water. A glass left full may later be found empty and the contents wetting the floor. A paper and pencil may be used by a ghost to leave bizarre marks or a legible message. Leave two stacks of coins—10 pennies in each stack—on a stable surface and leave the room for an extended period of time. When you return, the coins may be scattered. If both stacks are scattered, a gust of wind or vibration of the building may account for the change. If one stack remains untouched while the other is scattered, that may be the work of a ghost. I used this technique at the Myrtles Plantation in St. Francisville, Louisiana. I found 10 pennies rearranged in a circle around the other stack of coins, which remained standing.

Other Equipment

Various authorities in the field of ghost hunting suggest the following items to help you mark sites, detect paranormal phenomena, and collect evidence of ghostly activity.

White and colored chalk	Small bell
Compass	Plastic bags for collecting
Stop watch	evidence
Steel tape measure	Light-reflecting tape
Magnifying glass	Matches
First-aid kit	Tape for sealing doors
Thermometer	String
Metal detector	A cross
Graph paper for diagrams	Bible
Small mirror	Cell phone

THE PSYCHIC APPROACH

The Psychic Approach relies upon your intuition, inner vision, or emotional connection with a deceased person, object, place, or point of time in history. You don't have to be a trained psychic to use this approach. All of us have some capacity to tap into unseen dimensions and use some of the psychic tools described in the parapsychology literature and popular books by psychics such as Sylvia Browne, Annette Martin, and Jane Roberts. Your ability to use psychic tools for successful ghost hunting depends upon three factors: innate ability, receptivity, and sensitivity.

You may have an ability to successfully use psychic tools in a ghost hunt if you are one of those people who can readily identify isolated places within a room that give that chilling feeling that there is something bizarre or paranormal about the spot. The ability to identify these places must include a capacity to sort out your impressions, clear your mind of extraneous thoughts and distractions, and focus your attention on the particular point from which a paranormal impression emanates.

You may have sufficient receptivity to effectively use psychic tools if you feel more intensely connected to a place or past era than others or often feel mentally transported to another era. Do you often get that curious feeling that some unseen person is standing behind you, watching you, or touching you? When you touch an artifact, such as a weapon, do you get the impression that you have become aware of information about the object or its user? If so, you are receptive to unseen dimensions and likely to have success hunting ghosts with psychic tools. Highly receptive people often visit a place for the first time yet feel they have been there before. This is called ESP, or extrasensory perception, and reflects a high degree of receptivity.

Your receptivity can provide considerable focus to your ghost hunt if you first obtain information about the key elements and historical context of the entity's death. This includes architectural elements of a home, theatre, airplane, or ship and objects such as furniture, clothing, weapons, or any implement or artifact of the specific time period of the entity's death. Touching or handling pertinent artifacts, sitting in the deceased person's chair, or standing within the historic site will enable you to get in touch with the historical moment that is most pertinent to the ghost.

You may have exceptional sensitivity if you get vivid impressions of emotions in specific locations within allegedly haunted places. Do you walk into a historic building and get that eerie feeling that something or someone from the past still lingers there? Do you get a sense of fear, anger, pain, or suffering when you visit historic places or places known to be haunted? If so, you may be sensitive to residual energies from past events, emotions that played out in a particular place, or the actions of people who have been gone from the scene for decades. Sensitive people often detect a distant time or a voice, sound, touch, or texture of another dimension often described as a change in atmosphere.

Your sensitivity will pay off in a ghost hunt if your investigation is aimed at strong paranormal imprints or attachments of spirits. Strong imprints and attachments are indicated by the frequency, duration, and consistency of the paranormal event reported to occur at a particular place. The strongest imprints are created by intense emotions such as fear, rage, jealously, revenge, or loss, especially if they were repetitive over long periods prior to death. Strong attachments are created by love for a person, a place, or an object or a sense of obligation to provide guidance and protection. Biographical research may reveal this kind of information, particularly if personal letters or diaries are examined. Old newspaper articles, suicide notes, wills, and photographs are useful too.

You may enhance your sensitivity by developing and expressing empathy for the ghost's lingering presence at a haunted site. Empathy can be based on your research, which may reveal information about the entity's personal history and probable emotions, problems, or unfinished business at the time of death. You may also learn that a ghost may be trapped, confused, or have chosen to remain at a site to protect someone or guard something precious. Historical sources like newspaper articles and obituaries, old photographs, or biographies can help you discern the motivations behind the ghost's reluctance to move on.

Your sensitivity to ghostly environmental imprints and spirit manifestations may also be increased by meditation, the relaxing of one's physical body to eliminate distracting thoughts and tensions and achieve emotional focus. Meditation allows you to narrow your spiritual awareness to a single subject—a place, entity, or historic moment in time. Markers of time or season, artifacts or implements, furniture and doorways are a few suggestions of things to focus on. As the subject comes into focus, you can add information obtained from your research, information that relates specifically to the spirit under investigation such as the type of device used for a suicide or murder, favored book, musical instrument, etc. Through this process, you will become aware of unseen dimensions of the world around you, creating the feeling that you have moved through time to a distant era. Meditation gets you in touch with the place, date, and time pertinent to a ghost's imprint or death. It also enables you to disregard personal concerns and distracting thoughts that may interfere with your concentration on the ghost you seek.

Keep in mind that it is possible to be in a meditative state while appearing quite normal. The process is simple and easy to learn. When you arrive at the site of your ghost hunt, find a place a short distance away to meditate. Three essentials for any effective meditation are comfort, quiet, and concentration.

Comfort: Sit or stand in a relaxed position. Take free and even breaths at a slow rate. Do not alter your breathing pattern so much that you feel short of breath, winded, or lightheaded. Close your eyes if that enhances your comfort or focus on a candle, tree, or flower. Do not fall asleep. Proper meditation creates relaxation without decreasing alertness.

Quiet: Meditate in a place away from noises generated by traffic, passersby, radios, slammed doors, and the like. If you are with a group, give each other sufficient personal space. Some people use mantras, repetitive words or phrases, or speak only in their mind in order to facilitate inner calmness. Mantras are useful to induce a focused state of relaxation, but they may disrupt the meditation of a companion if spoken aloud. A majority of ghost hunters do not believe that mantras are necessary in this instance. They point out that ghost hunting is not like a séance as depicted in old movies. It is not necessary to chant special words, call out to the dead, or invite an appearance "from beyond the grave."

Concentration: First, clear your mind of everyday thoughts, worries, and concerns. This is the most difficult part of the process. Many of us don't want to let go of our stressful thoughts. To help release those worries, let the thought turn off its light and fade into darkness. After you clear your mind, some thoughts may reappear. Repeat the process. Slowly turn off the light of each thought until you can rest with a completely cleared mind. This might take some practice. Don't wait until you are on the scene of a ghost hunt before you practice this exercise.

Once your mind is clear, focus on your breathing and imagine your entire being as a single point of energy driving the breathing process. Then, open yourself. Think only of the entity you seek. Starting with the ghost's identity (if known), slowly expand your focus to include its personal history, the historical era of the ghost's death or creation of the emotional imprint, the reported nature and appearance of the haunting, and any specific ghostly activity.

Acknowledge each thought as you continue relaxed breathing. Find a thought that is most attractive to you and then expand your mind to include your present surroundings. Return slowly to your current place and time. Remain quiet for a minute or two before you resume communication with your companions, then move ahead with the ghost hunt.

Psychic Tools

Clairaudience: The impression of sounds generated by paranormal sources may be perceived through clairaudience. The term is derived from the French, meaning "clear hearing." People with this ability may hear the voices of spirits who are trying to communicate or the sounds of events that occurred years or decades earlier. The latter are environmental imprints most often created by intense repetitive emotions or an occurrence that had a strong emotional component.

Clairsentience: Some ghosts manifest by creating impressions of physical sensations such as being touched. Others are accompanied by fragrances or odors. The ability to perceive or detect physical sensations and smells that do not truly exist on this plane is called clairsentience. Signature perfumes or the fragrance of favorite flowers can help you identify a ghost. At the world-renowned haunted Myrtles Plantation in Louisiana, the ghost of Sara Woodruff creates the fragrance of her favorite flower, the magnolia. Odors such as cigars, oranges, and hemp are common ghostly manifestations. Sometimes, ghost hunters encounter the noxious odors of rotting meat or burning flesh.

Clairvoyance: Information or impressions may be received from objects or spirits without the use of "normal" senses. The process is called clairvoyance and usually refers to visual impressions. People who see ghosts, whether the image is lifelike or merely a human-shaped fragment of a shadow, are clairvoyant. Visual information or impressions may include orbs, amorphous clouds, or shadowy objects. Since clairvoyance is limited to "real time" events, any visual experience suggests a ghost is present at the moment.

Retrocognition: Visual perceptions of events or places from the past is a form of clairvoyance called retrocognition. Psychic Derek Acorah dramatically portrayed his retrocognition ability during ghost investigations on the popular TV show *Most Haunted*. If you watched my show *Ghosts of the Queen Mary,* you've seen me perform retrocognition. The most famous case of this type of clairvoyance was reported by two teachers, Charlotte Moberly and Eleanor Jourdain, after they visited the Petit Trianon at the Palace of Versailles in France in 1901. In what has become known as the Moberly-Jourdain incident, the women reportedly witnessed people dressed in 17th-century clothing and saw structures that no longer exist. Their detailed descriptions of the experience, published in their 1911 book, *An Adventure,* match obscure historical records, suggesting the retrocognitive experience was genuine. Detailed accounts of the Moberly-Jourdain incident can be found online.

Psychometry: Information about an object or one of its users may be obtained by psychically gifted or skilled people through psychometry. First described in 1842 by Joseph R. Buchanan, the process has been used in séances, ghost hunts, and crime scene investigations. After a few minutes of handling an object, practitioners of psychometry receive visual impressions or become aware of information that cannot be the result of logical inference (piecing things together from clues you might have). Ghost hunters can use psychometry to gain information about a spirit's affinity for a chair or a book or why it moves a particular item. Any object that has reportedly been moved by a ghost should be examined by psychometry. Investigators may get clues about the identity of the ghost or reasons for its haunting activity.

Retrieval of information by psychometry may be possible because of changes in an object's electromagnetic field (EMF) created by repetitive handling. Its owner's use may have altered its EMF and left durable traces of the user's energy, much like a fingerprint, especially if intense emotions were associated with frequent use. A good example is my Civil War cavalry saber, which was used in several battles. Psychometrists who handle the saber become aware of fear, rage, and remorse and perceive the image of a middle-aged Union army officer.

GROUP ORGANIZATION AND PREPARATION

It is not necessary to believe in spirits or paranormal phenomena in order to see a ghost or experience haunting activities. Indeed, most reports of ghost activities are made by unsuspecting people who never gave the matter much thought. However, you should not include people in your group who openly express negative attitudes about the paranormal. If you include skeptics, be sure they agree to maintain an open mind and are willing to participate in a positive group attitude.

Keep your group small, limited to four members if possible. Ghosts have been seen by large groups of people, but small groups are more easily managed and likely to be of one mind in terms of objectives and methods.

Meet an hour or more prior to starting the ghost hunt at a location away from the site. Review the history of the ghost you seek and the previous reports of spirit activity. Discuss the group's expectations, whether they are based on known or suspected ghostly activity or specific research goals. Review any available reports of audio phenomena, still or video images, and visual apparitions and decide what methods would be optimal for recording these phenomena during your investigation.

Most importantly, agree to a plan of action if a sighting is made by any member of the group. The first priority for a ghost hunter is to maintain visual or auditory contact without a flurry of activity, such as making notes. Without breaking contact, do the following: activate recording devices; redirect audio, video, or photographic equipment to focus on the ghost; move yourself to the most advantageous position for listening or viewing the ghostly activity; attract the attention of group members with a code word, hand signal (for example, touch the top of your head), or any action that signals other hunters so they can pick up your focus of attention.

Should you attempt to interact with the ghost? Do so only if the ghost invites you to speak or move. Often, a ghost hunter's movement or noise frightens the ghost or interferes with the perception of the apparition.

SEARCHING FOR GHOSTS

There are no strict rules or guidelines for successful ghost hunting except *be patient!* Professional ghost hunters sometimes wait several days, weeks, even months before achieving contact with a ghost. Others have observed full-body apparitions when they least expected it, while concentrating fully on some other activity. Regardless of the depth of your research or preparation, you need to be patient. The serious ghost hunter will anticipate that several trips to a haunted site may be required before some sign of ghostly activity is observed.

If you are ghost hunting with others, it may be advantageous to station members of your group at various places in the ghost's haunting grounds and use a reliable system to alert others to spirit activity. In the event that even one member sights a ghost or experiences some evidence of ghostly activity, confirmation by a second person is important in establishing validity and credibility. In the previous section, a hand signal (hand to the top of the head) was recommended as a means of informing others that they should direct their eyes and ears to a site indicated by the person in contact with a ghost. Because of this, all ghost hunters need to keep their companions in sight at all times and be aware of hand signals.

An audio signal can often reduce the need for monitoring other ghost hunters for hand signals. Equally important for a group is to establish a method for calling other hunters who may be some distance away, as when each member patrols a different portion of the site. Tugging on a length of string can be an effective signal. So can beeping devices, mechanical "crickets," and flashing penlight signals, i.e., one flash for a cold spot and two flashes for an apparition. Hand-held radios, or walkie-talkies, can also be effective. Some models can send an audio signal or activate flashing lights. Cell phones can be used but the electromagnetic activity may be uninviting to your ghost.

Remaining stationary within a room, gravesite, courtyard, or other confirmed location is often most productive. If a ghost is known to have a favorite chair, bed, or other place within a room, he will appear. Under these conditions, the patient ghost hunter will have a successful hunt. If your ghost is not known to appear at a specific place within a room or an outdoors area, position yourself to gain the broadest view of the site. A corner of a room is optimal because it allows the ghost unobstructed motion while avoiding the impression of a trap set by uninvited people who occupy his favorite space. If you are outdoors at a gravesite, for instance, position yourself at the base of a tree or in the shadows of a monument to conceal your presence while affording a view of your ghost's grave. If your ghost is a mobile spirit, moving throughout a house, over a bridge, or about a courtyard or graveyard, you may have no choice but to move around the area. Search for a place where you feel a change in the thickness of the air or a cold spot or detect a peculiar odor.

Once you are on site, the above-described meditation may help you focus and maintain empathy for your ghost. Investigate sounds, even common sounds, as the ghost attempts to communicate with you. Make mental notes of the room temperature, air movement, and atmospheric sensations as you move about the site. Changes in these conditions may indicate the presence of a ghost. Pay attention to your own sensations or perceptions, such as the odd feeling that someone is watching you, standing close by, or touching you. Your ghost may be hunting you!

WHAT TO DO WITH A GHOST

On occasion, professional ghost hunters make contact with a ghost by entering a trance and establishing two-way communication. The ghost hunter's companions hear him or her speak, but the ghost's voice can only be heard by the trance communicator. Sylvia Browne's book *Adventures of a Psychic* describes several of these trance communication sessions. Most ghost encounters are brief with little opportunity to engage the entity in conversation. But the ghost may make gestures or acknowledge your presence through eye contact, a touch on the shoulder, sound, or a movement of an object. The ghost hunter must decide whether or not to follow the gestures or direction of a ghost.

While driving the back roads of the Santa Lucia Mountain, near

Big Sur, and the Santa Cruz Mountains, travelers have encountered the ghosts of hitchhikers. These lifelike beings disappear soon after entering the car. There is no truth to the rumor that the experience has caused drivers to have accidents.

Phantom miners have been spotted in the Santa Cruz Mountains at Almaden near San Jose and south of Big Sur. Those who have encountered these grizzly-looking, lifelike spirits were shaken, but they suffered no ill-effects.

Visitors to historic buildings in Monterey, Carmel, and San Luis Obispo often feel the touch or tug of a ghost on their arm or shoulder. Spirits of deceased prospectors, miners, or outlaws at New Almaden or San Juan Bautista may be trying to get living souls to notice them, move out of their way, or follow them to some important destination.

A ghost at Santa Cruz Memorial Park cemetery, on Graham Hill Road, believed to be a veteran of World War II, points to the location of a grave. Many who have seen this fellow wonder if he has lost his own grave or wants to be moved close to that of a family member. Near Paso Robles, the ghost of a woman walks the grounds of Adelaida Cemetery. She has a bright, misty appearance that startles many visitors who go there simply to capture orbs in their pictures. At many of the Spanish missions, the unmarked graves of hundreds of Indians create intense cold spots and a frightening sensation of being pulled downward.

On a road between Santa Ynez and Solvang, a phantom coach speeds by unsuspecting people. A driver sits atop the large black coach, holding the reins that control four black horses. Some witnesses have been so startled by this phantom that they stop in the middle of the road, creating a traffic hazard.

At Missions San Miguel, La Purisima Concepcion, and San Carlos de Borromeo, in Carmel, candles carried by shadowy figures resembling monks in long robes entice witnesses to follow them to sites where Indians are buried in unmarked graves.

On Fisherman's Wharf and nearby Del Monte Beach in Monterey, the ghosts of drowning victims appear. Some of them are spotted in the water and appear to be living beings in real distress as they repeat their death event. Witnesses have called 911 seeking help.

The idea of a close experience with a ghost is frightening to most of us. More often, the ghost's activities are directed at getting the intruder to leave a room, house, or gravesite. If you sense your ghost wants you to leave, most hunters believe it is best not to push your luck. When you have established the nature of the ghost activity, ascertained that your companions have experienced the activity, taken a few photographs and run a few minutes of audio tape, it may be time to leave. An experience with an unfriendly ghost can be disturbing.

Residents of haunted houses and employees of haunted business establishments often accept a ghost's telekinetic or audio activities without concern. It is part of the charm of a place and may add some fun to working in a spooky building.

AFTER THE GHOST HUNT

Turn off all recorders and remove them to a safe place. Some ghost hunters suspect that ghosts can erase tapes. Label your tapes with the date, time, and location. Use a code number for each tape. Keep a separate record of where the tape was made, date, time, and contents. Place tapes in a waterproof bag with your name, address, telephone number, and a note that guarantees postage in case it is misplaced. Have photographic film developed at a professional color laboratory. Pros at the lab may help you with cropping and image enhancement. Have copies made of the negatives that contain ghostly images.

All members of the group should meet right after the hunt, away from the site. Each hunter who witnessed ghostly activity or apparition should make a written or audio statement describing the experience. The form presented in Appendix A should be completed by the group leader. Video and audio recordings made at the site should be reviewed and reconciled with witness statements. Then, plans should be made for a follow-up visit in the near future to the site to confirm the apparition, its nature and form, and the impressions of the initial ghost hunt.

Data about the ghost's location within a site may indicate the optimal conditions for future contact. Things to be aware of include the time of day or night, phase of the moon, season, and degree and size of cold spots, as well as form and density of the apparition. Patience and detailed records can help you to achieve the greatest reward for a ghost hunter, unmistakable proof of ghostly activity.

CHAPTER 2

The North-Central Coast:
San Mateo Coast, Santa Cruz, and Capitola

California's coast may be divided into several distinct geographic regions, each with a name or artificial boundaries that may not fully describe the land, panorama of the Pacific Ocean, or the backdrop of majestic mountains. It is true to say, however, that between Moss Beach and Santa Cruz, Highway 1 conveys travelers 90 miles through a desolate, beautiful, and fascinating north-central coast that contains numerous uninhabited beaches, vast stretches of green and golden-hue pastures, and densely wooded mountains still populated with mountain lions, bobcats, and deer. With a few lonely lighthouses, historic villages, and remnants of pioneer homes, this coast is also populated with many ghosts. A unique regional history of 18th-century Spanish exploration, 19th-century Mexican and Yankee settlement, several natural catastrophes, and manmade disasters has left us with several haunted places. Separated from the congested San Francisco Bay Area by coastal mountains traversed by only a few narrow roads, a visit to the north-central coast is a unique experience that offers many opportunities for encounters with ghosts and other forms of paranormal activity.

SKYLAWN MEMORIAL PARK

Highway 92 West at Highway 35
San Mateo 94402
650-349-4411

Highway 92 makes a long, sweeping, horseshoe-shaped curve in front of Skylawn Cemetery. In bad weather, this portion of the highway is hazardous, especially for those driving too fast on motorcycles. Slippery pavement has generated a lot of business for this cemetery. Tired travelers, driving home from a day at the beach in nearby Half Moon Bay, have also contributed to the graveyard's population.

The ghost that haunts this portion of Highway 92 is not linked to Skylawn Cemetery, but she is attached to the intersection with scenic Skyline Boulevard. I've visited this beautiful graveyard during daylight hours, and at night, and found little evidence of anything paranormal. Ghosts seldom appear in cemeteries unless their grave is defaced by vandals, damaged by natural phenomena, or desecrated. I've seen a few neglected graves at Skylawn but none that would arouse the indignation of a spirit and lead to a ghostly presence.

The Skylawn ghost is a female believed to be the victim of a horrific accident that occurred at the intersection of the highway and Skyline Boulevard in 1972. A car driven by a drunk driver crossed the center-line and collided with several motorcycles, killing four people. The Skylawn ghost may have been a passenger on one of the motorcycles. She shows up late at night, at the site of her death, seeking a ride home. Startled eastbound travelers see her sitting in the back seat of their car wearing a leather jacket. It is said that she looks anxious or stressed but pays no attention to the car's occupants. This apparition appears for only a few seconds and then vanishes. The residual odor of wet hair has been noticed by some witnesses.

I know this story sounds like a common urban legend in which a ghost appears in the back seat of a car as it passes by a graveyard or site of an accident. I might have dismissed it as such myself except a friend, who happened to be a 20-year veteran of the San Mateo County sheriff's department, told me he experienced the Skylawn ghost. Late one night, while transporting a prisoner from Half Moon Bay to San Mateo, the handcuffed man in the back seat began whimpering as the car passed the Skylawn Cemetery. When the deputy sheriff turned around to quiet the prisoner, he saw the transparent image of a young woman in the back seat. Her pale, frightened face was framed with brown hair that appeared wet or matted with blood.

GHOST OF THE BLUE LADY

Moss Beach Distillery
Beach Way at Ocean Boulevard
Moss Beach 94038
650-728-5595

Several publications and TV shows have placed the Moss Beach Distillery among America's top ten haunted places. Since the 1970s, many famous paranormal investigators have visited this location and described its ghosts. Psychics have channeled the victims of criminal activity and picked up on remnants of torrid emotions and tragic deaths. Paranormal experts such as Sylvia Browne, Loyd Auerbach, Richard Senate, Stache Margaret Murray, Neva Turnock, Annett Martin, and Japanese psychic Aiko Gibo have affirmed that the place is haunted.

In the summer of 2008, the investigation team from the Atlantic Paranormal Society (TAPS) visited the Moss Beach Distillery. Entering the famous haunted restaurant with high expectations, TAPS investigators astounded the paranormal community when they discovered several electronic devices mimicking paranormal activity. Among these "paranormal re-creation" devices was a radio-controlled motor that caused a ceiling lamp to swing, audio devices that created disembodied voices and other sounds, and a projector that created the blue-tinged face of a woman in a restroom mirror. Many viewers of the TAPS TV show *Ghost Hunters,* who were familiar with the considerable technical expertise of these investigators, were amazed that the restaurant's management would use these devices to trick seasoned ghost hunters into concluding the Moss Beach Distillery was haunted. The site's longstanding reputation, and very active ghosts, would have likely resulted in TAPS concluding that the building is, indeed, haunted.

The decision of the restaurant's management to install devices to simulate paranormal activity severely damaged the decades-old reputation of the restaurant. Many people now wonder if the highly publicized ghost stories about the distillery ever had any credence. I can tell you that I've had many encounters with paranormal phenomena

During Prohibition, this restaurant was a speakeasy that attracted bootleggers and others who now haunt the place, including the famous Blue Lady.

at this location that match up with reports made in the 1970s, '80s, and '90s. Most of my experiences occurred before the lower level was remodeled and paranormal re-creation devices were installed. So, is this place truly haunted? My experience points to the conclusion that ghosts and hauntings, or environmental imprints, may be discovered throughout the building.

At least three ghosts haunt the Moss Beach Distillery. Historical research and investigations by gifted psychics have identified two women and a man who may have been involved in a lover's triangle. They were part of a group that hung out in the 1920s and '30s at Frank Torres' speakeasy, Frank's Roadhouse. Located on a cliff overlooking a secluded part of the San Mateo coast, Frank's place was perfect for Canadian bootleggers who landed boats on the beach and dragged kegs of whiskey up the cliff for storage in the roadhouse basement. Some of this contraband was sold on the site to silent-movie stars, politicians, and others from the San Francisco Bay Area who came for a weekend of partying at a time when the sale of alcoholic beverages was illegal. The place also attracted dangerous characters whose clandestine activities included murder.

With the repeal of Prohibition in 1933, business at Frank's Roadhouse increased with the sale of legal drinks and development of a fine restaurant. A hotel located across the street accommodated guests who chose to include sex in their wild weekends on the coast. It is known that one of these encounters ended with a murder.

The most famous ghost at the Moss Beach Distillery is called the Blue Lady. Legend says that she had an affair with the roadhouse piano player, John Contina, a swarthy romantic who used his musical talent to attract women to his room. The true identity of the Blue Lady is uncertain, but research, particularly channeling performed by renowned psychic Sylvia Browne, points to three possibilities. On November 13, 1919, Mary Ellen Morley was killed in a horrific automobile accident on the coast highway. Married with a young son, she died at the scene, a few hundred yards from a small bar and brothel that preceded the construction of Frank's Roadhouse. The Blue Lady may be Anna Philbrick, a jilted lover of Contina who may have been responsible for his murder.

Psychic Annette Martin believes the Blue Lady is the ghost of Elizabeth Clair Donovan. During channeling, this spirit insisted that her nickname, Cayte, be used. Cayte reported that she moved from the Midwest to San Francisco with an abusive husband. Breaking from him, she found comfort with the romantic John Contina. Eventually, her husband discovered her whereabouts, confronted her inside the roadhouse or on the beach, and killed her. Contina met his death on the beach at the hands of his other girlfriend, Anna Philbrick.

According to legend, Contina's most amorous and public relationship was with a woman who showed up almost every night dressed in a blue chiffon dress. Psychics who have contacted this spirit report that the lady loves the color blue but sometimes dresses in a contemporary basic black cocktail dress. This ghost also expressed her happiness that Frank's is still in business and filled with people who like having spirits around.

For nearly four decades, reports of paranormal activity have been made by surprised and unbiased guests, employees, paranormal investigators, and TV production teams. This list of ghostly activity is too long to include in this book, but reports include moving objects such as swinging ceiling lights, glasses on the bar, bottles moving off the shelf, chairs and boxes sliding across the floor, and doors that open and close by unseen hands. One astonished guest reported a table knife turning by itself. Calling for the attention of nearby guests and a waiter, several people confirmed that the objects moved by unseen forces. On several occasions, heavy bar stools have flipped over.

Several reports of objects becoming airborne have been made, too. Employees Byron Whipp and Patty McKeller witnessed a stack of bill folders move horizontally off a shelf to the center of a wait station and then drop to the floor. Former owner Pat Andrews sat in her office, astonished, as a checkbook rose from her desk and floated around the room as if an invisible being were carrying it.

Ghosts of the Moss Beach Distillery like to play with electrical devices. At times, the restaurant's thermostats have reprogrammed with nonsensical start and stop times. Televisions and lights turn on and off, sometimes in the middle of important local football games. The restaurant's phone system is a frequent target for ghosts. At times, repeated calls are answered only to find that the caller refuses to speak. Orders for wine that were not made by patrons have showed up on the bar's computer. One night, all transaction dates showed up with the year 1927 instead of the current year.

These antics are fascinating, but most paranormal enthusiasts who visit the distillery want to see a ghost. Many have not been disappointed. Children as a young as four years old have spoken of seeing a Blue Lady standing in the bar, restaurant, or lobby. Boys have run from the restroom to report a lady "in the wrong room." Children in the neighborhood used to speak of a Blue Lady who chased them away from the steep cliff adjacent to the restaurant. People walking the beach below the distillery have reported seeing the Blue Lady, a woman dressed in black, a man covered with bloody wounds (probably John Contina), and a rough-looking fellow in seaman's clothes with a gun in his hand, likely one of the bootleggers from Canada who landed contraband whiskey on the beach.

Paranormal investigator Loyd Auerbach had an unusual encounter with the Blue Lady in the bar. While noting spikes on his EMF meter, Auerbach felt the female spirit pass through his body. This event was witnessed by three psychics who detected the passage of the spirit through living flesh. Auerbach reported that sharing his space with a ghost "felt pretty good."

Numerous séances conducted at the distillery have established connections with spirits who related their reasons for haunting the place. The piano player, John Contina is still looking for women, including the lady who killed him on the beach. The Blue Lady loves the place and feels comfortable with renovations and the modern crowds of patrons. In spite of doubts cast by the TAPS discoveries of devices that "re-create" paranormal activity, the place remains spiritually active. When I stopped in for coffee late in the afternoon on November 14, 2008, the place was jammed with customers. Business at the bar suddenly slowed and patrons became edgy as bartenders announced the computer system had failed to accept charges from the bar. One longtime employee leaned toward me and whispered, "Must be those spooks you're looking for."

NEGLECTED GHOSTS

Pilarcitos Cemetery
Highway 92
Half Moon Bay 94019

A few steps past the gate of this historic, derelict graveyard and visitors forget about the noisy traffic on busy Highway 92. Crumbling monuments, epitaphs eroded by the passage of 150 years, depressions in the ground indicating unmarked graves, and masses of dense fog caught in tall trees give this place a spooky atmosphere even when the sun shines. The first graves were opened here in 1820 when the town was known as San Benito, then Spanishtown as more Yankees settled in the area. They eventually renamed the town Half Moon Bay. As the community developed, with an influx of Irish, Portuguese, and German immigrants joining the Spanish and Mexicans already established there, a Catholic church was constructed in 1856 at the edge of the graveyard. The structure was destroyed by a fire in 1870, leaving no trace.

Many of the founders of Half Moon Bay are buried in Pilarcitos Cemetery, but their graves are hard to find. At dusk, and into the evening, you might encounter their spirits, though. So many of the graves have been damaged by weather, vandals, and some of the homeless who illegally camp there that spirits have returned to look after them. Unexplained lights have been spotted by ghost hunters and surprised passersby. At several gravesites, EVP have been recorded that include sobbing, groaning, a woman's voice humming, and occasional admonitions to "Get out" and "Leave." All of this points to the conclusion that the spirits of the cemetery are saddened by the neglect of the grounds, trash that accumulates, and damaged headstones.

I've experienced some amazing paranormal phenomena at the grave of Bridget Trowell. Born in Ireland in 1830, this woman immigrated to America during the potato famine and ended up in Half Moon Bay. She was probably amazed at the similarities between the green pastures of her new community in America and the seaside farms of her native Ireland. Her bliss did not last as long as hoped; she died at the age of 40 on January 15, 1870. The sea air has eroded engravings on Trowell's impressive headstone, but it is apparent that her family held her in high esteem. I suspect her decedents gathered at her grave for decades, mourning her demise with intense emotion. Environmental imprints of their grieving are strong and easily detected by sensitives.

If you plan to visit Pilarcitos Cemetery, make a preliminary visit in daylight to become familiar with the grounds and locate specific graves you can target in your investigation. Return at dusk or early evening to look for ghost or other paranormal phenomena, but only if you are accompanied by another person who can enhance your safety. Be aware that homeless people sometime camp in the graveyard, and they do not like to be surprised by visitors.

GHOSTS OF THE OLD TOWN

Half Moon Bay Inn
401 Main Street
Half Moon Bay 94019
650-726-1177
www.halfmoonbayinn.com

The beautiful Half Moon Bay Inn is the centerpiece of the historic Main Street business district. Surrounded by several old buildings housing tourist-oriented businesses, the inn is an alluring sight, having recently undergone a yearlong renovation. Fascinating artifacts from the inn's history and architectural elements from other locations have anchored a few ghosts to the building.

Sebastian Belli constructed the two-story building, with a large basement, in 1932 to serve as a hotel, family residence, and ice cream parlor. During recent renovations, several horseshoes were found at the foundation of the building. Research revealed that a blacksmith's shop once stood on the property.

Two large doors salvaged from San Francisco's famous Cliff House open from the restaurant to the courtyard. Records indicate the doors date from 1908 and were installed during reconstruction after the San Francisco earthquake of 1906. For nearly a century, the high society of the city, and some visiting presidents, passed through these beautiful doors, grasping the brass handles and, perhaps, leaving behind a trace of energy. Sensitives who pass through these doors report the muted conversations of a crowd of people even when the restaurant of the Half Moon Bay Inn is empty.

During the 1940s, the inn was a popular destination for troops stationed on the coast. On weekends, dances with live bands rocked the place, as soldiers and their sweethearts had their last rendezvous before the boys shipped out to war. For many soldiers and sailors, their last night in Half Moon Bay might have been their final taste of happiness. As such, the pale apparition of a soldier has been seen roaming the halls of the second floor. He doesn't bother anyone nor does he make any sound or move objects. He merely walks the halls, looking into rooms when the doors are open. He might be looking for the girl with whom he spent his last night before dying in the war.

At one time, the basement of the inn housed a casino operated by a Chinese family. The business was legal, but stories about the casino suggest the place was not operated fairly. At times, when the owners saw that the house was losing, a waiter was ordered to set off strings of firecrackers. Frightened by the noise and smoke, winners scraped their money from the tables and raced out, saving the owners from more loses. The basement is not generally open to visitors, but ghost hunters may be granted permission to look around, do an EVP sweep, and take some pictures. The apparition of a skinny Chinese man has been seen rushing through the basement. He appears to be wearing an apron.

Other apparitions and paranormal phenomena at the Half Moon Bay Inn suggest the ghost of Mrs. Belli and her daughter may still be on the premises. Mrs. Belli operated the Greyhound Bus Station in the building while her daughter, Sylvia, ran the ice cream parlor.

The latest round of renovations was completed in January of 2009. Typically, ghosts are more active after a building undergoes renovation.

JOHNSTON HOUSE

Highway 1 at Higgins-Purisima Road
Half Moon Bay 94019
650-726-0329
www.johnstonhouse.org

I doubt that anyone associated with the Johnston House Foundation will discuss the possibility that this historic home is haunted, but I believe it is. Standing alone, in the middle of a large field sweeping upward from the ocean, the New England-style "salt box" has survived high winds, damp weather, vandalism, abandonment, and the passage of 150 years. At one point during reconstruction of the building's foundation, strong winds caused the two-story structure to collapse into a pile of hand-hewn redwood beams. Thanks to the hard work of the Johnston House Foundation, the place has been beautifully restored giving visitors an opportunity to see what life was like on the coast in 1855 when Half Moon Bay was known as Spanishtown.

James and Petra Johnston built the house and raised their four children there with the help of Petra's mother, Melita Valenzuela de Jara, who came from Mexico to assist her daughter. But the ghost that haunts this place was not a member of the family. A Chinese cook, listed in the 1860 regional census as "Sam Chinaman, aged 22," may be the ghost I've detected in the kitchen and back rooms of the house.

Sam arrived in San Francisco from Canton, China, in the late 1850s, and somehow made his way down the coast to Spanishtown.

Benevolent James Johnston hired him to cook for his family and hired hands, called drovers, who cared for the sheep and dairy cows raised on the property. Sam became so loved by the family that Petra became his godmother, and he was baptized a Catholic on May 30, 1861. This may have been an essential step for Sam as he married the Johnston's nursemaid, Crescensia.

It is not known how long Sam remained employed at the Johnston house, where he died, or the date of his death. It is likely that he was buried in nearby Pilarcitos Cemetery, but his name is not on the list of recognized graves. Recollections of visitors recorded in letters and other sources indicate that he was working at the house in the 1880s.

I've sensed Sam's presence in the kitchen and back rooms of the first floor. During my last visit to the house, I walked about accompanied only by a docent who offered historical information. Standing quietly in the kitchen, I smelled the aroma of cooked food and heard feet, clad in leather slippers, shuffling about on the redwood floor. I did not capture valid EVP, but I recommend that ghost hunters use this mode of investigation in the Johnston House kitchen.

Upstairs, in a small room now labeled the exhibit room, a perfumed presence was detected. Melita may have used this room as a bedroom. The small room between the master bedroom and the exhibit room

Built in 1855, the Johnson House was nearly demolished by high winds, but it stands today, restored and haunted.

has been restored as a chapel. However, it was likely used as a nursery, and Crescencia probably slept there as she cared for the Johnston children.

GHOST OF THE LIGHT KEEPER

Pigeon Point Lighthouse
210 Pigeon Point Road
Pescadero 94060
650-879-2120

Pigeon Point Lighthouse has stood on this wind-swept, rocky promontory since 1872. When its lard oil lamp was lit for the first time, on November 15, and its flame illuminated the 1,008 prisms of the Fresnel lens, a beam of light was cast more than 20 miles over the sea. Mariners sailing along the coast between San Francisco and Los Angeles relied on this lighthouse to maintain a safe distance between their vulnerable wooden ships and the rocky San Mateo County coast. Still, there were several shipwrecks in the vicinity. Some of the survivors sought refuge at the Pigeon Point Lighthouse, their only beacon when storms raged on the coast.

The ghost spotted at this lighthouse is not one of the survivors of the many shipwrecks that occurred in the area. He appears to be one of the lighthouse keepers who served there. Some have reported that this man wears a keeper's cap with a distinctive emblem. The keeper's house at the base of the 115-foot tall tower is currently off limits to visitors pending restoration, but witnesses standing at the fence have seen this fellow emerge from the door, descend the steps, walk to his left around the corner of the house toward the fog-horn barn, and then vanish.

I have seen the ghost of the keeper several times over a period of 20 years. After diving for abalone in the rough waters off the point, I often walked past by the keeper's house to get to my car. In most sightings, I noticed the man, dressed in a dirty blue uniform, go down the steps and walk toward the ocean. Cold and tired from diving, I did little more than notice the man and nod to acknowledge his presence. On occasions when I watched him walk his route, I was astonished

Pigeon Point Lighthouse stands on a fog-shrouded promontory and attracts shipwrecked spirits.

when he vanished before my eyes. The first sightings I dismissed as the result of hypothermia and fatigue. Later, I spotted the man, walking the same route, before I started my dive.

Recently, I've returned to the lighthouse specifically to look for the keeper's ghost. The house and tower are worn severely from the harsh coastal climate, but the ghost is still there. Visitors and guests at the adjacent youth hostel occasionally spot the ghost as he leaves his stone and stucco cottage to walk toward the sea. All of my sightings of the keeper's ghost have been in daylight, but this part of the coast rarely has bright sunshine. Low overcast and fog add to the spooky ambience of this desolate place.

Guided history tours of the lighthouse are offered Friday through Sunday. The youth hostel offers lodging within view of the keeper's house.

GHOSTS OF OLD DAVENPORT

St. Vincent de Paul Catholic Church
Davenport Jail
Site of Old Davenport
Highway 1 at Davenport Avenue
Davenport 95017
831-429-1964

This quaint, little town 11 miles north of Santa Cruz is a popular destination for surfers, cyclists, hikers, bikers, and other travelers attracted to the rugged beauty of the coast. Ghost hunters target this destination, too, because several spirits roam the town.

The largest building in Davenport is the St. Vincent de Paul Catholic Church, constructed in 1915. Its beautiful interior is often used as a venue for art classes, but the grounds are a good site for ghost hunting. For decades, people have reported seeing pale apparitions of men and women passing in and out of the church. These apparitions may be environmental imprints created by emotionally charged churchgoers. I've been told that ghosts of several people sometime appear simultaneously, resembling a crowd leaving the church after worship services or a funeral. Curiously, these apparitions are most common in the morning, on days when the sky is overcast or dark from foul weather. I've found no reports of EVP at this location, but audio investigation near the church doors would likely capture evidence of something paranormal, such as spoken words, the singing of hymns, or the sound of organ music.

Not far from the church, the old Davenport jail stands on a tiny street behind Phipps Gallery (450 Coast Road, Highway 1). Constructed in 1914, the jail is one of the oldest buildings in town. There is no record of anyone dying in the two-cell structure, but it has been the target of ghost investigations. In fact, the jail was used for only 22 years before it was abandoned. In 1987, the local historical association took it over and converted the tiny building to a museum. Filled with artifacts from the region's history, it is possible that some ghosts came along with historical objects gathered from Davenport homes and businesses that no longer exist.

Odd noises have been detected emanating from the jail in the evening. I've received reports of singing, two men arguing, a metal cup slamming against the wall, and a drum. Access to the building at night might be impossible, but EVP may be captured at the rear window.

The original site of Davenport is on El Jarro Point, one mile north of the present town center. In 1868, Capt. John P. Davenport built a large house on the point overlooking the 450-foot-long pier he constructed and operated as a major shipping facility. The house no longer exists, but the captain and his wife raised 10 children there. Men who labored to build the pier stayed on as longshoremen or opened shops, bars, and hotels in the settlement, which was known as Davenport's Landing.

Little remains of the original buildings at this location, but sensitive visitors detect a foul odor on the beach that cannot be recognized. Dismissing various sources such as a sewer outfall or rotting kelp on the beach, I was told by an elderly resident that the odor is that of whale blubber as it is boiled to render oil. It turns out that a large whaling station was established in Davenport in the 1870s. Some of the large cauldrons used to boil blubber can still be found in the area. I doubt that physical remnants of spilled oil would exist on the beach and create the odor detected by sensitives. This finding is a paranormal remnant; however, I do not know why the boiling of whale fat would create such an environmental imprint.

GHOST OF THE OLD SAILOR

Red, White, and Blue Beach
5021 Coast Road (Highway 1) at Scaroni Road
Santa Cruz 95060
831-423-6332

This beautiful beach and privately operated campground was a popular destination for nudists and clothed visitors for many years, but it closed in 2006. It reopened in September 2009 as a clothing-optional recreation area, but visitors are not allowed to carry cameras. The access road to the beach was once marked with a red, white, and blue mailbox, hence the name of the place; it has since been replaced by a nondescript gray box to discourage visitors. When visiting, look for Scaroni Road. This crescent-shaped dirt road joins Highway 1 at two points.

A two-story Victorian house, built in 1857 by a retired sailor, stands at the entrance to the beach and campground. It has been reported that the ghost of the old sailor, dressed in a rain slicker and broad-brimmed hat, strolls out the back of the house to make his rounds through the campground and then on to the beach. There are times when the sailor appears upset by the large number of people walking the grounds of his home and parking vehicles on the once quiet dirt road connecting his small estate with Highway 1. Residents and visitors have reported seeing objects fly from tables and shelves, as if thrown by invisible hands; disembodied footsteps; the sound of breaking glass when no disturbance can be found in the house; and doors slamming. This ghost also likes the beach kept clean. Astonished witnesses have seen discarded cans and bottles take flight toward trashcans.

In their books about haunted places, writers Randall Reinstedt and Antoinette May recount the story of the residents who moved into the house in the 1950s. A few days after unpacking their belongings, the family members found a well-worn rain slicker and hat hanging from a peg near the back porch. They were unaware of its significance until weeks later when they spotted a pale apparition on the beach wearing the rain gear. Since the 1950s, at least a dozen reports have been made each year of the ghostly sailor, wearing a slicker and hat, walking about the beach or campground.

There may be other spirits haunting this beautiful beach. In 1986, a psychic and ghost hunter witnessed an unusually thick fog roll onshore. Moments later, a huge black bird, possibly a turkey vulture, emerged from the fog and hovered over her head as an evil presence settled over her. This experienced ghost hunter reported that she was "scared to death."

GHOST OF SARAH COWELL

The Haunted Meadow
Cowell College
University of California, Santa Cruz campus
Santa Cruz 95064

The colleges that comprise the University of California, Santa Cruz are scattered across rolling hills that once belonged to local millionaire Henry Cowell. Having made a fortune in the 1860s by mining lime, a commodity required for the manufacture of bricks, Cowell raised his three daughters and two sons on thousands of acres of land that offered magnificent views of the ocean and isolation from the bad elements of society. His children enjoyed all the advantages his great wealth could provide, but as adults, he limited their social experiences and even forbade them to marry. Sarah Cowell (1863-1903) and her brothers and sisters found great pleasure and adventure on the ranch, though, with magnificent redwood groves for hiking and broad meadows for buggy rides and picnics.

On May 14, 1903, an afternoon buggy ride across the ranch should have been a delightful experience for Sarah and her companion, a housekeeper. Spring flowers had turned the green meadows into a sea of amazing colors, and the breezes from the ocean were fresh with a hint of salt. After hours of traveling over the sprawling ranchlands, something spooked the tired horses, causing the buggy to overturn, turning an afternoon delight into an awful tragedy.

Sarah was thrown to the ground, fracturing the bones of her neck. Ranch hands carried her to a nearby house where she lingered for one hour before dying. The grieving family transported her body to San Francisco in a chartered railroad car where a lavish funeral sent her off to heaven. There is evidence, however, that Sarah did not move on. Long before the University of California's colleges were constructed on Cowell ranchlands, the place where Sarah died was known as Haunted Meadow. The small house in which she took her last breath was demolished long ago, but Sarah still strolls through the meadow, enjoying the ocean breezes and wild flowers. Her ghost appears in the afternoon and early evening, usually in the shadows cast by tall trees. She appears to be wearing a long, pale yellow gown and a hat or bonnet. This ghost seems oblivious to witnesses and does not create a frightening atmosphere.

Sarah's sisters, Helen (1865-1932) and Isabella (1857-1950), were so shaken by the lost of their beloved sister that they vowed never to return to the ranch. Since they were unmarried women, the sisters moved to a mansion in Atherton, on the San Francisco peninsula, and never traveled to Santa Cruz again. Their aversion to their once beloved home invites speculation that something about the place frightened them. When Helen died in the Atherton mansion in 1932, Isabella had the house destroyed and the rubble enclosed by a fence. Perhaps Isabella blamed her sister's death on spirits that had followed them from Santa Cruz.

When Isabella died in 1950, her will directed that her San Francisco mansion be destroyed. Clearly, Isabella felt that something in her three homes was implicated in family tragedies.

The Haunted Meadow lies east of Cowell College. Topographic maps show it as Pogonip Park. The meadow may be accessed by taking Highway 9 from central Santa Cruz to Golf Club Drive. At the end of the drive, an information kiosk at the ranger station indicates the foot-route to the Haunted Meadow Trail. From Cowell College, hikers may start at Glenn Coolidge Drive and take Lime Kiln Trail to the Haunted Meadow Trail.

GHOST OF LILY

Student Ghosts
Porter College
University of California, Santa Cruz
Santa Cruz 95064

Universities located in rural areas can be hotbeds for rumors about student suicides and other tragic deaths. I've investigated many of these and found that more than 90 percent of the rumors could not be verified through newspaper reports or police records. Some private universities keep students' deaths secret because they fear unfavorable publicity that may reduce alumnae support. At UC Santa Cruz, I discovered several rumors and a few interesting stories.

Near Porter College, the ghost of a homeless girl named Lily has been spotted walking the well-worn paths of a small meadow near the provost's residence. It is said that she died of exposure in the 1970s, when the university was under construction. I asked several students about Lily's ghost. All of them agreed the story was true but only two admitted they had seen her. I questioned a construction worker who has been involved in a nearby building project for two years. He reported that he saw the ghost of a small, frail woman walking the meadow on several occasions. She always appeared dressed in a simple garment, which the man described as a long white T-shirt. He was certain the woman was a ghost, because even on cold, windy days, she appeared to be wearing only a T-shirt as she walked 30 to 50 feet before vanishing.

Buildings A and B of Porter College may be haunted by the ghosts of students who died there or other entities. In building B, some unoccupied rooms are dubbed the "Bermuda Triangle." A resident assistant told me there have been reports of objects flying across these rooms and bizarre noises. Some who have entered the rooms reported that they felt they were in the presence of a malevolent spirit. Sorting through the varied and sometimes excessively enthusiastic reports of students, I became suspicious that a poltergeist, not a noisy ghost, but an emotionally disturbed living being, may have created paranormal activity. A poltergeist might also be responsible for frightening students who wake up feeling they are being strangled.

In building A, a student suicide is reportedly responsible fore the apparition of a young man who has been seen walking the hallways of the fifth floor. Reports I obtained were varied, but all of the people I interviewed agreed that the ghost is dressed in dark pants and a white shirt.

GHOST OF JENNIE JETER

Cliff Crest Bed and Breakfast Inn
407 Cliff Street
Santa Cruz 95060
831-427-2609
www.cliffcrestinn.com

Named for its prominent location in Santa Cruz's beach hill, the Cliff Crest Bed and Breakfast Inn has been known for decades as a haunted house. Built in 1887 for attorney William Thomas Jeter (1850-1930) and his wife, Jennie (1859-1959), the building has undergone numerous renovations through the years, but its 19th-century character has been beautifully preserved. Will's political activities eventually earned him a job as lieutenant governor of California. Due to Governor Budd's poor health, Will performed the duties of the state's chief executive, occasionally working from his Cliff Street home. Will is better known for using his political power to protect the Santa Cruz County Big Trees Park, known as Big Basin, which contains one of the largest stands of redwood in California. The 2,000-year-old Jeter Tree, named in Will's honor, marks the grounds he fought to preserve.

Through his illustrious political career, Will was supported by his devoted and nurturing wife, Jennie. After Will died, Jennie lived another 29 years in the Cliff Street house, sleeping in a room now called "Jennie's Room." Surrounded by mementoes of 45 years with Will and other comforting memories, Jennie died in this room. In spite of a succession of other owners, there are indications that Jennie is still attached to the room and its former furnishings.

For decades, employees working on the first floor have heard footsteps coming from Jennie's room above them. Often, the footsteps ended with the sound of furniture being dragged across the floor. When employees hurried to the second floor to investigate, no one was found who might be responsible for the sounds.

Jennie also likes to rearrange pillows on the bed. Staff members have often found their careful placement of pillows disturbed. Many times the pillows would resemble a horseshoe, an arrangement that would offer support to both arms as a person reclined on the bed.

The ghost of Jennie Jeter still walks the rooms of this old house, which is now a bed-and-breakfast inn in Santa Cruz.

As she approached her 100th birthday, Jennie might have been comforted by the pillows placed under her arms to help take the stress off her arthritic shoulders. Ghost hunters who stay in Jennie's room should use this information to entice a ghostly appearance. An audio recorder left on during a long absence from the room might capture disembodied sounds of moving furniture.

The ghost of Jennie Jeter is said to generate a pleasing sense of relaxation. People who stay in her room have reported an almost miraculous dissipation of their stress.

STACKS OF GHOSTS

Sunshine Villa
80 Front Street
Santa Cruz 95060
831-459-8400

In 1860, the Kittredge family built a gothic mansion on a vacant lot no one else seemed to want. Situated on the backside of Beach Hill, a house at this spot would provide no views of the ocean nor would it receive cool breezes from the sea. Added to that, the land was said to be sacred to local Indians and covered in a veil of mystery. It was unclear if the site was used as a burial ground or merely for religious ceremonies. Still, the Kittredges built their three-story mansion complete with gables, peaked roofs, and bay windows.

Within 10 years, the family was gone from their rundown home and the place was opened as the McCrary Hotel. By 1900, it was a flophouse for drunks and vagrants who wandered the beach during the day. After World War II, when property near the beach became more valuable, the mansion was renovated and reopened as a resort. Today, the restored Kittredge house stands as the main building of a complex known as the Sunshine Villa Assisted Living Center. Modern upgrades have not diminished its old reputation as a spooky place.

For many years, employees and visitors have reported intense and unexplainable cold spots, moving shadows, eerie noises, and suspicions that Indian spirits and the spirit of a murder victim occupy the place. Many people have seen mysterious blue lights float down darkened corridors. Members of the night staff have heard the voices of women calling out for help but are unable to locate anyone in need.

Since this building has a sordid history spanning more than 60 years, it is uncertain what events might have caused so many spirits to become attached to the building. There is no available record of a murder at this location, but in the late 1800s, when the building was a seedy hotel or flophouse, such a crime could have taken place without much public notice.

If this structure looks familiar, it's because the great director Alfred Hitchcock was inspired by its architectural features when he created the eerie Bates mansion for the movie *Psycho*.

GHOST OF ANGEL AGNES

Golden Gate Villa
924 Third Street
Santa Cruz 95060

One hundred years after the tragic death of Agnes McLaughlin, her ghost walks the halls of the spectacular Golden Gate Villa, confused and shocked by the awful thing her stepfather did to her. She produces inexplicable cold spots, which defy the blazing sunshine of summer days, and a cozy feeling that an unseen being is watching as the current residents enjoy the comforts of the huge mansion. At times, Agnes also creates an atmosphere of sadness punctuated with bursts of sobbing and anger directed at her killer.

The great Golden Gate Villa was built in 1891 for Maj. Frank W. McLaughlin, a retired army officer who made and lost a number of fortunes in mining operations. It is reported that his friendship with Thomas Edison and membership in the Republican National Committee also fattened his bank account, giving him, what he thought, was a secure financial future. To round out his life, he built a grand mansion on Santa Cruz's beach hill and moved in with his new bride, Margaret Loomis, who had been widowed at a young age, and her 17-year-old daughter, Agnes. It is said that Frank quickly grew to love the charming young lady and adopted her.

Agnes was known as one of the most beautiful young ladies in Santa

Cruz, but few people saw her outside of church, when she was seen traveling to and from the church in a carriage. Frank closely regulated Agnes's social life even as an adult.

In the 1890s, the family enjoyed an exceptional lifestyle in the 10,500-square-foot palace. Ornate carved woodwork, seven fancy fireplace surrounds, and large rooms illuminated by huge chandeliers decorated with gold leaf made Frank feel that he could receive and impress his important friends in a luxurious style. Among the notables he entertained in this house are Theodore Roosevelt and Sarah Winchester.

Everything seemed to be going well for Frank until November 16, 1905, when his wife died. This tragic event was soon followed by huge financial losses that left him feeling defeated and isolated from his high-rolling friends. For two years, he and 34-year-old Agnes lived quietly in their home on beach hill.

One Sunday, Agnes returned home from church and went to her room to rest. After loosening her corset, she reclined on her bed. Sometime that afternoon, Frank entered her room, held a gun to her head, and pulled the trigger. Mortally wounded, Agnes died at 6:00 P.M.

The ghosts of murder/suicide victims Agnes McLaughlin and her father, Frank, are believed to walk the halls of this Santa Cruz mansion.

A short time after the murder, Frank retired to his room and poisoned himself with potassium cyanide. When the contents of his suicide note were leaked to the local newspaper, rumors flew about town that the murder/suicide had little to do with Frank's recent financial loses. In the note, he is quoted as saying, "I love her so, and so I take her with me." This sentence led to speculation that Frank had romantic feelings for his adopted daughter and was tortured by the impropriety of his desires. Current owner of the house, Patricia Wilder, insists that we should not misinterpret Frank's statement.

In an interview with writer Sarah Phelan, Wilder said, "The major was undoubtedly possessive of Agnes, but he adored his wife. The story of why he killed her has always been cast in a negative, but can't people think in a different light? Agnes was so little when the major married her mother that she became his child; he cared about her only in that way."

This defense hasn't deterred speculation by people who can't imagine why a man would kill someone so dear. It is possible that Frank's mental state deteriorated to the point of irrationality. In the suicide note, Frank requested that the family doctor chloroform the cat to finish the dissolution of his family.

A stained-glass window in the staircase contains a likeness of Agnes. This image may be the link through which the murdered woman remains attached to her beloved mansion on the hill. Legend says that locks of her golden hair were mixed with the coloring agent for glass.

FUJI RESTAURANT

(Formerly Best of China Buffet)
525 Water Street
Santa Cruz 95060
831-427-0182

Named for a mountain in Japan, this Chinese restaurant occupies a building that was once home to Adolph's Restaurant and the short-lived Best China Buffet. Unlike its predecessors, the Fuji has received some great reviews and a steady flow of regulars who are sold on the quality of food and service. Years ago, employees of Adolph's Restaurant reported frequent and highly disturbing paranormal activity in the kitchen, restrooms, and near the buffet. Being greatly unnerved by the ghostly presence, they contacted the Santa Cruz office of the famous Berkeley Psychic Institute and asked for help ridding the place of the belligerent spirit. The staff reported seeing a tall male figure dressed in a long, black coat and a hat reminiscent of the 1940s. Witnesses claimed he scowled and groaned as he moved about the kitchen. At the buffet, he caused stacks of plates to slide into a pile, with some falling to the floor.

None of the Fuji Restaurant's personnel I talked with knew any of the Adolph's employees. According to a waiter and a busboy at Fuji, the paranormal activity, including sightings of a tall, dark figure, continues, but it is not frequent nor does it disturb the staff.

No one at the restaurant knew anything about the history of the building that might point to the identity of the ghost or its reasons for haunting the place. The building does not look very old. The architectural style is typical of 1970s family-style restaurants; however, it is possible a portion of the structure was once part of a much older building. In the 1920s and '30s, Water Street was lined with card rooms and other establishments that may have served illegal liquor in secret bars called speakeasies, which were sometimes run by tough characters. The ghost of the Fuji Restaurant might have been a bouncer, enforcer, or someone involved with bootleg liquor.

GHOST OF THE MISSION PADRE

Mission Santa Cruz
144 School Street
Santa Cruz 95066
831-425-5849

Visitors to this part of Santa Cruz might think of it as cathedral hill. The tall steeples of the imposing 1880s vintage Catholic church, the plaza and small park used for outdoor gatherings on Sunday, and the tiny Spanish mission resemble promontories in other cities, such as San Francisco and Seattle, that are also known by this moniker. Locals, however, call this place *haunted hill.*

In 1769, Spanish soldiers and priests climbed this hill and noted how it stood high above the sea, offering protection from the French and Russians and the periodic floods of the nearby San Lorenzo River. They planted a wooden cross on the crest of the hill and erected a mission, which was consecrated August 28, 1791. Local Indians from the Ohlone, Quiroste, and Yokut tribes were drawn to the mission by the kindness of mission priests, but they were eventually enslaved. Harsh treatment of the Indians by mission fathers led the Quiroste tribe to attack the mission on December 14, 1793. Partially destroyed, the mission was rebuilt within a year.

Another attack occurred October 13, 1812. Angered by Father Andres Quintana's liberal use of a metal-tipped whip, mission laborers beat him to death and disfigured his body by smashing his testicles with stones from the church's foundation.

The Spanish Mission Santa Cruz opened its doors in 1771 and was the scene of an Indian attack in 1793.

The terrible pain of his torture has left Father Quintana's ghost to wander haunted hill. Some say he is looking for the Indians who killed him to forgive them. Regardless of his motivation, his apparition, dressed in brown robe and sandals, appears menacing. Those who live in the neighborhood often see him in the park in front of the church or inside the mission. Some longtime residents of the area with whom I talked reported their ancestors had passed on stories of the Spanish priest and his frequent appearances on haunted hill. He has been seen walking quickly, taking long strides, across the park. He has also been seen inside the mission near the altar.

TOTALLY CREEPY

Rispin Mansion
Clares Street at Wharf Road
Capitola 95010

The best way to describe this derelict mansion is "totally creepy." The place has been officially closed to the public since it was abandoned in 1956, but anyone who walks by, or spends a little time peaking through the chain-link fence at the massive structure, gets the foreboding feeling that something scary is looking back or reaching out with menacing fingers. Developers have obtained the city's permission to convert the weathered structure to a fancy bed and breakfast inn, but it is hard to imagine that any renovation will rid the place of its reputation for ghostly activity.

San Francisco-based petroleum executive Henry Allen Rispin built the 7,000-square-foot, four-story mansion is 1921, just two years after he managed to purchase nearly all privately held land in Capitola. Seeking to develop a community composed of huge summer homes for the moneyed society of the Bay Area, Rispin poured all his resources into his dream of making Capitola the "Newport" of the West Coast. The venture ultimately failed, and by 1929, Rispin was broke. The 22-room mansion passed through the hands of several owners, some of whom used it for nefarious purposes, including the storage of bootlegged rum during Prohibition. In1940, the Oblates of St. Joseph purchased the building and turned it into a convent. The holy order lasted only

16 years before they abandoned the place, citing a persistent chill in many of the rooms and unwanted attention from the surrounding community. For the next 30 years, the mansion was stripped of woodwork, windows, and doors and occupied by hippie groups who raised goats and vegetables, scribbled graffiti on the walls, and fostered the notion that bizarre things were occurring in the old house.

Aside from rumors of drug sales and wild pot parties, stories are still told of rumrunning Mafiosi from the 1930s, murders allegedly occurring in the basement, sequestered kidnap victims, rapes, and satanic rituals staged in the chapel. Most of these stories cannot be verified.

When asked about these rumors, Carolyn Swift, director of the Capitola Museum, said, "That stuff drives me crazy. There's no truth behind any of it, except maybe the rumrunning." But if you ask longtime residents of Capitola, many recall high-school days when they broke into the place to smoke, drink, and party only to be scared away by something very weird that they could not explain.

Spiritualist Sara Harvey insists there is "some bad juju in there." She has offered her services to developers to rid the place of both good and bad spirits to ensure the new inn's success.

Among the spirits residing in the Rispin Mansion is a short, slim woman dressed in a long, black gown. Some have reported her wearing

Numerous ghost sightings and other paranormal experiences have been reported at the Rispin Mansion. These apparitions may be the result of wild parties and criminal activity conducted at the home that led to fatalities.

a wide-brim hat and a veil, similar to a Victorian mourning bonnet of the late 19th century. This ghost appears to be searching for something in a third-floor room. There are reports of secret rooms and cabinets throughout the mansion that were used to hide valuables.

On the main floor, a man wearing glasses has been seen standing next to a fireplace. He appears to be enjoying the warmth of burning logs in a fireplace that is now clogged with ashes. There is speculation he is Henry Rispin, savoring the remnants of his once great dream.

A young man and his vicious dog roam the dark recesses of the basement. Police used to train attack dogs in the area. This ghost also shows up at the front door. In the former chapel, disembodied screams and moans are heard.

When I last visited Rispin Mansion in January of 2009, there was no legal access except by permission of the developer. Standing at the fence at night, though, witnesses have seen strange lights moving throughout the house and heard muted calls for help. Ghost hunters should watch for the opening of this place as a bed and breakfast and be among the first to spend a night there. Ghosts are usually most active after major renovations.

CAPITOLA THEATRE

120 Monterey Avenue
Capitola 95010
831-462-3131
www.bslopera.com

The Capitola Theatre sits within spitting distance of priceless beachfront property, yet it looks as if it has been waiting for the wrecking ball for 10 years. Weathered by salt air and the passage of more than 60 years, the theatre has served as a movie house and, more recently, a venue for opera.

During its conversion from a movie house to a stage theatre, construction workers often heard the intangible voices of a large crowd of people milling about the lobby or walking down the aisles. At times, when all work ceased, the place filled with the sounds of a large audience. These sound phenomena lasted only a few seconds, but they were loud and repetitive, sometimes occurring 10 times in an hour.

The voice of a woman believed to be a seamstress had been heard coming from the area where the projection booth is located. She may have used that room to repair costumes. It has been reported that the female sounded like a former owner who died in 1997.

The building has been used only occasionally over the past five years. Sitting so close to a beautiful beach, there is pressure to replace it with a luxury hotel. In my experience, theatre ghosts don't give up on the site they haunt. Their passion for the stage and desire to be admired by a large audience keeps them on site even after the building has been demolished.

49 GHOSTS

Brookdale Lodge and Spa
11570 Highway 9
Brookdale 95007
831-338-4770

The historic Brookdale Lodge and Spa sits like a gracefully aging matriarch, tarnished and a bit a rundown, but still offering glimpses of her once celebrated beauty and hints of her notorious past. She stands surrounded by the massive redwoods that played a role in her history, brought wealth to her door, and gave strength to her structure, allowing her to stand for 140 years. Today, she is miles from the nearest major highway but still an enormously popular destination for people looking for adventure or respite in the glorious Santa Cruz Mountains. She is also a venue for paranormal enthusiasts who come in search of her 49 ghosts.

The first building on the site was opened in 1870 as headquarters for the Grover Lumber Mill. The mills and offices were located on the south side of Clear Creek while bunks houses and dining hall for lumberjacks were constructed on the north side. A small footbridge connected the facilities. When the mill closed in 1900, Judge James Harvey Logan bought the property and converted the buildings into a hotel and campgrounds. Over the years, subsequent renovations enclosed the creek within a huge dining room that accommodated as many as 200 people. Rustic but beautiful, with massive boulders, natural redwood beams, ferns, and exotic birds in large cages, the

Brookdale Lodge became internationally known in the 1920s as the foremost retreat on the West Coast for movie stars and gangsters. Among the well-known patrons were Marilyn Monroe, Tyrone Power, Rita Hayworth, Alfred Hitchcock, Shirley Temple, and Pres. Herbert Hoover.

During periods of decline, the remote location of the lodge attracted bootleggers and rumrunners who supplied illegal liquor to patrons in the San Francisco Bay Area. Murders, missing persons, tragic drownings, fires, and other mysterious events have contributed much to the legends and lore of Brookdale Lodge and offer insight into the presence of so many ghosts.

The most famous of the Brookdale ghosts is eight-year-old Sarah Logan, niece of the lodge's developer, Judge Logan. In the 1920s, little Sarah was playing at the edge of Clear Creek when she slipped and hit her head on a rock. Falling unconscious into a few inches of water, she drowned. It wasn't until the 1940s, however, that stories of a ghost girl began circulating. Reports have accumulated over the past 60 years that describe the lifelike image of a slim, blond girl wearing a blue and white knee-length dress tied about her waist with a cloth belt. She has been spotted at the edge of the creek, near the four-sided fireplace in the bar, running through the lobby, and playing on the balcony of the Brook Room. A tearful Sarah has approached some visitors, asking for the whereabouts of her mother.

Nestled in the Santa Cruz Mountains a few miles from the ocean, the Brookdale Lodge was once a favorite destination of Hollywood movie stars and mobsters.

I encountered the ghost of Sarah Logan when I was 10 years old. My family used to spend time at the Brookdale Lodge. During one of our visits, I wandered away from my father and brother, climbed down the rocks to the creek, to hunt for frogs. While mesmerized by the trickling waters, pollywogs, and fish in the stream, I sensed that my six-year-old sister had joined me at the water's edge. As I scanned the stream, I felt her press close to me and I wondered how she had climbed down the steep embankment without help or making any noise. At that moment, my mother called to me from the patio above, demanding that I get away from the water. As I looked at her, I was stunned to see my sister standing hand in hand with my mother. Looking around, I saw no one else near me.

Five years later, I came across a magazine article about the Brookdale Lodge and the tragic story of Sarah Logan. The account led me to believe that I had had an encounter with the young girl's ghost at the site where she drowned. After I became a ghost hunter, I returned to the lodge many times and spotted Sarah near the four-sided fireplace and in the bar facing the glass wall of the swimming pool.

The ghost of Sarah's mother has been seen in the massive Brook Room, too. She appears wearing a long skirt, high-collared blouse, and her hair gathered in a large bun on the back of her head. She has been seen standing with little Sarah, overlooking the creek where her daughter drowned.

The ghost of another girl, a 13 year old who drowned in the swimming pool, haunts the bar. She died in 1972 and shows up often. A glass wall allows patrons seated at the bar an underwater view of the pool. Her apparition appears as though it is a reflection as she stands a few feet away from the bar.

The prevalence of gangsters at the lodge during the 1930s through early 1950s led to murders and disappearances that have been linked to ghostly activity. A mysterious tunnel running under the street and a former meat locker, sealed to visitors, are believed to be places where gangsters killed men who had betrayed them. It is said that the victims' bodies still lay beneath the lodge. In room 46 of the new wing, much of the poltergeist-like activity has been attributed to these victims whose remains rest in unmarked graves.

The ghost of a lumberjack appears in the lobby, in the bar known as the Mermaid Room, and near the double doors that open to the Brook Room. In the Fireside and Pool Room, music remnant of the big-band era has been captured on audio and video recorders. Short bursts of brass instruments and drums have been identified as 1940s-style music.

In the new wing, built over the site of A. J. Logan's campground and rustic cabins, guests have reported strange sounds, lights, cold spots, and frightening contact with invisible forces. Room 46, in particular, has been the site of frequent, intense poltergeist-like activity that includes objects flying about the room. There have been many reports of images of dancers floating through the room, sometimes making eye contact with the astonished occupant.

The Brookdale Lodge has been featured on many television programs and videos that may be useful to ghost hunters who want to research this location before visiting. Some of these include fascinating interviews with employees and guests. Psychics who have visited the lodge believe there may be as many as 49 ghosts roaming about the historic landmark. Check with the lodge for a schedule of ghost-related meetings and events.

THE WHITE FIGURE

Santa Cruz Memorial Cemetery
1927 Ocean Street (at Graham Hill Road)
Santa Cruz 95060
831-426-1601
www.scmemorial.com

With a few exceptions, spirits of dead people rarely haunt cemeteries. Ghosts may show up at their gravesites if the monument or headstone is defaced or damaged. They might also visit the fresh grave of a loved one, looking for the deceased person they've missed. For these reasons, ghost hunters are advised to target damaged or new graves for EVP sweeps and video surveillance. Typically, the paranormal phenomenon detected in cemeteries is comprised of environmental imprints created by intense, repetitive emotions experienced by living people who visit a gravesite frequently. No ghosts are present, but the audio and photographic evidence of something paranormal can be spectacular.

There are reports of a highly active, belligerent ghost at Santa Cruz Memorial Cemetery. This ghost has been described as a white figure not clearly discernible as male or female. The figure moves quickly, floating a foot or so off the ground. People who enter this cemetery at night report that the ghost flies toward them as if to frighten them into turning around and leaving. There is no information about the identity of this ghost, but there is speculation that, when alive, he or she worked at the cemetery as a caretaker because the entity appears wearing coveralls and holding a shovel.

Visitors have also reported seeing orbs and faces in the headstones. Unexplained dark shadows fall across the paved roads and bizarre noises have been heard, sounds clearly not made by animals such as frogs and cats.

Santa Cruz Memorial Cemetery opened in 1862 and burials continue. When I visited the place in December of 2008, four fresh graves were being dug. Many veterans of America's wars are buried there, including several who fought in the Civil War. The cemetery is huge and covers nearly 100 acres of rolling hills. I advise a daytime visit to become familiar with the place and identify a few key gravesites for your investigation. Be aware that the white figure usually shows up as soon as you enter the cemetery, but it has been known to harass ghost hunters as they continue roaming about the grounds.

GHOST OF THE MUTILATED MOTORCYCLIST

Highway 9, 0.4 miles north of Boulder Creek
Boulder Creek 95007

Serpentine Highway 9 is a thrill ride for many motorcyclists traveling over the *hump* from the Silicon Valley to the coast. Coursing through tall redwoods, the two-lane road is shrouded in shadows most of the way, creating an almost surreal pathway that seems to encourage daredevil driving. One young man from my hometown died on Highway 9 on April 4, 2008, when he crossed the centerline, only four-tenths of a mile from the edge of Boulder Creek, and slammed into the front of a northbound pickup truck. According to witnesses, the motorcyclist was traveling at a high rate of speed and did not appear to see the on-coming truck. He may have been distracted by the sharp curve of the road or the splash of sunlight that penetrated the thinning trees.

During the hours required for clearing the wreckage, traffic on Highway

9 was at a standstill. A newspaper account told of more than fifty motorcyclists who were halted at the site by accident investigators. Many of them reported that viewing the terrible scene was a sobering experience.

Soon after the April 4 accident, travelers on Highway 9 began reporting a man who staggered alongside the road, heading south to Boulder Creek. Often, drivers caught only a glimpse of the man as their attention was focused on driving the winding road. As a passenger, a friend of mine passed through the area a month after the accident. He reported seeing a man dressed in a leather jacket and motorcyclist's chaps standing at the edge of the road. The man appeared to notice passing vehicles, even holding out his hand as if he were thumbing for a ride. As my friend's truck moved closer to the man, he vanished. The image was clear enough, however, that a massive head wound was apparent.

The ghost has been spotted at any time of day. Ghost hunters who investigate this location should do so cautiously. A position on the shoulder of the northbound lane will offer full view of the accident sight while allowing safe clearance from traffic.

An interesting sidebar to this story: as sheriff's deputies cleared the body and wreckage from the highway, two hikers emerged from the woods and reported they had discovered a skull. Over the past 20 years, several skeletal remains have been discovered in the Santa Cruz Mountains that were ultimately linked to high-profile criminal activity in the San Francisco Bay Area.

Other places to hunt ghosts:

GHOST OF THE CITY COUNCIL

IOOF Hall
526 Main Street
Half Moon Bay
650-712-0718
www.halfmoonbaymemories.com/category/ioof/

This two-story building has been the Ocean View Lodge of the IOOF since 1868. At that time, the town was named Spanishtown. The building has also served as a meeting place for the Masons, Sons of Italy, Boy Scouts, and the local 4-H Club. Modern businesses, including the M Coffee shop and Tokenz, an arts and crafts store, occupy the ground floor. The second floor, though, remains much as it was in the 1870s. The 19th-century décor and artifacts from the earliest days of the IOOF Lodge create a fascinating ambience and have contributed to widely held suspicions that the place is haunted. All five members of the first Half Moon Bay city council were members of this lodge. Perhaps one of them has remained in the lodge where most of the city's political decisions were made.

WHITE COCKADE SCOTTISH PUB

18025 Highway 9
Boulder Creek 95006
831-338-1414

This popular watering hole was closed in the summer of 2007. When I last visited Boulder Creek in December 2008, the building was for sale. The place has been renovated, but it has yet to reopen. The Scotch motif remains in place and fits in with the highland topography of its surroundings. Bartenders who worked there used to tell stories about shot glasses flying through the air, bottles falling to the floor, lights flickering, and strange, ethereal grunts emanating from some unseen being behind the bar. This paranormal activity has been attributed to an old lumberjack named Ben who may have lived on the site when logging was the area's major industry. Another spirit, named Barbara, haunts the women's restroom and back bar. When the place reopens, ghost hunters should stop in while traveling to other haunted sites in the Boulder Creek area.

NOISY GHOST

Zaballa House
324 Main Street
Half Moon Bay 94019
650-726-9123

The owners and staff members of this bed and breakfast refuse to confirm or deny that ghostly activity occurs in any of the guest rooms. Being the oldest house in Half Moon Bay, suspicions run high with the belief that events occurring here over the past 150 years have led to some intense paranormal phenomena. Published reports suggest room 6 is haunted by the spirit of a person who died in that room. No personal history of the house's occupants in the 19th and 20th centuries is available to identify ghost-generating events or the identity of persons who may be haunting the place. A guest book once kept in the room comprises a record of several bizarre experiences, including rattling windows on nights when the air is still, broken objects such as keys and glasses, and activation of the smoke alarm.

SHADOWBROOK RESTAURANT

1750 Wharf Road
Capitola 95010
831-475-1511
www.shadowbrook-capitola.com

The most active ghost of this famous restaurant is that of Englishman E. O. Fowler who built the first structure on this site. The rustic log cabin he constructed at the edge of Soquel Creek was intended to be a summer home for his family. By the 1930s, however, the family had moved on and the place was abandoned. Its derelict appearance, nearly overgrown by dense foliage along the creek, and bizarre experiences of neighbors who occasionally ventured into the place led to its reputation as a haunted house. In 1947, the large log structure was rescued from further decay by a group of businessmen who opened Shadowbrook Restaurant. Several rounds of stunning renovations have culminated in spectacular décor, earning this restaurant a reputation as one of the most romantic on the coast. The ghosts, including E. O. Fowler and at least three others, are reported to be friendly.

LOVE CREEK LANDSLIDE

Vineyard Lane, past the intersection with Love Creek Road
Ben Lomond 95005

On January 3, 1982, a 500-year storm brought torrential rains, which saturated a steep hillside overlooking Love Creek in the Santa Cruz Mountain hamlet of Ben Lomond. At 1:00 A.M. on January 5, the hillside gave way and 5 million cubic meters of earth slid into the creek, damming the swollen stream. Floodwaters engulfed houses along the waterway not buried by the landslide. Twenty people died in this disaster, and many of the bodies were never recovered. Today, houses dot the steep hillside on Vineland Road, where the slide occurred. Below, along Love Creek, ghosts of some of the victims wander near the water, perhaps searching for their bodies.

PURISIMA RUINS

Verde Road at Purisima Creek Road
Half Moon Bay 94019

The only ghost town in San Mateo County is really not recognizable as a town, but several remnants and some ghosts can be found at Purisima. Spanish soldiers founded the little hamlet before 1820 as an outpost for Mission Dolores in San Francisco. The lush land, ample water, and sunny climate supported the farms that supplied the mission with food. After the American annexation of California in 1846, the town continued as a farming center for booming San Francisco and other Bay Area cities. Prosperity derived from the land, however, eventually became less important than the ready access to the ships that found safe anchorage a few miles north at Spanishtown. By the later 1880s, Purisima was abandoned, leaving some of the area's prominent citizens in a cemetery overgrown by poison oak. The town's structures were destroyed by winter storms or salvaged for building materials used elsewhere on the coast.

Today, the graveyard, marked by crumbling tombstones with nearly unreadable epitaphs, and a few stone foundations of former buildings are all that remain of Purisima. Ghosts have been reported at the cemetery, though. They may be looking for their bodies in unmarked graves or hoping to get someone to clean up the old cemetery.

CHAPTER 3

The Monterey Bay Area: Watsonville, Monterey, Pacific Grove, and Carmel

The Monterey Bay Area is a world-renowned locale of great history stretching back to 1603 when the Spanish explorer Sebastián Vizcaino sailed into the crescent-shaped bay and claimed the land for his king. Settlement began in 1770, and many structures exist today that take ghost hunters back in time two centuries, offering encounters with the ghosts of Spanish *padres,* soldiers, and pioneers. In the city of Monterey, more than 40 buildings erected before 1850 are in use as inns, restaurants, museums, places of worship, and stores. Aside from offering visitors modern amenities, many of them have a ghost or two. Some of these places are described in great detail in Richard Henry Dana's classic historical account of his visit to Monterey in 1836, *Two Years Before the Mast.* Pulitzer Prize-winning author John Steinbeck added a more contemporary mystique to Monterey and its fabled Cannery Row in his classic novels *Cannery Row* and *Sweet Thursday.* Ghost hunters will also find fascinating haunted places in Watsonville, Moss Landing, and Carmel that may appear familiar. Local director and Carmel resident Clint Eastwood has made several films in this region.

GHOSTS OF THE ANGRY MEN

Redman House
Beach Road and Lee Road
Watsonville 95077

For many years, I taught scuba diving in Monterey and surfed in

Santa Cruz. Passing between these two locations hundreds of times, I couldn't help but notice the huge Redman mansion sitting amid a strawberry field with no comparable buildings nearby. For as long as I can remember, the place has been deserted, slowly decaying in the marine air and blasted by winter storms coming ashore at Pajaro Beach less than two miles away. I never saw anyone enter or leave the place nor have I seen a single vehicle parked near the porch. Dark and weathered, the house always gave me the impression that it was a phantom, not physically there but making frequent appearances from some other realm of existence.

The house was built by renowned architect William H. Weeks, the same man who designed the haunted Monterey Hotel. James Redman paid Weeks $3,368 to build the 6,000-square-foot Queen Anne-style Victorian farmhouse. The tall and imposing structure was the greatest house in the area, with interior finishes of eastern oak,

Ghosts haunt this derelict house as it slowly decays in the salt air blowing inland over the Pajaro Dunes of Watsonville.

bird's eye maple, and natural hardwoods. Interior lights were fueled by acetylene gas while several fireplaces warmed the place.

By the 1930s, the last of the Redman family had vacated the house, and the property was sold to the Hirahara family. This family of dedicated agriculturalists owned farmlands throughout the region until the bombing of Pearl Harbor in 1941. They, along with other Japanese families in the Watsonville area, were forced from their home and relocated in internment camps for the duration of World War II. During the war years, the property was maintained by friends of the family, often acting anonymously to avoid engendering ill-will within the local community.

After the war, the Hiraharas returned and converted their barn into housing for other Japanese Americans who struggled to rebuild their lives in their former community. Soon after the Loma Prieta earthquake of 1989, the house became unoccupied. In 1998, a group of Pajaro Valley residents formed the Redman House Committee and launched a campaign to restore the grand old mansion, which had become a regional icon. Today, the huge house sits on steel beams, jacks, and silts, awaiting the reconstruction of its foundation.

Several ghost hunters and others who have visited the abandoned house have discovered orbs in their photographs of the place. Light anomalies observed on the roof include flashes of white light and blue mist moving slowly across the disintegrating shingles. Visitors who have gotten as close as the cyclone fence allows claim they've heard doors slamming, the screams of a little boy, and adults shouting as though a huge argument raged within.

My own experiences are just as bizarre. During one of my trips between Monterey and Santa Cruz with a surfing buddy, we stopped to take a closer look at the mansion. Arriving minutes after sunset, the place was dark and foreboding. While ascending the steps, we both heard angry male voices emanate from behind the front door. As we stepped onto the porch, a massive gust of cold air seemed to blast through the sealed door and pass through us. The gust crossed the porch and descended the stairs, carrying with it the on-going din of angry voices. That was the only time I ran from a ghost.

DEL MONTE BEACH

The beach extends 4 miles east from the Commercial Pier of Monterey
  to Sand City
Casa Verde Way at Del Monte Avenue
Monterey 93440

A fog that seems to close out the modern world often shrouds this long, wide beach. In fact, many people come here to wander the open space and get away from their busy lives. At any time of day or night, when the fog rolls in or overcast skies hover low, ghosts emerge to walk the sandy shore of Monterey Bay, one of the few places in California where large numbers of ghosts have been at the same time. As many as 16 full-bodied, ethereal ghosts have appeared on this beach. What is more amazing is that four people witnessed these large gatherings of spirits. That group included three of my surfing buddies and me in 1979. The ghosts appeared to be male, possibly sailors or fishermen, dressed similarly in gray pants and shirts streaked with mud or grease. All of them had nondescript faces. They appeared to emerge from the dissipating fog as the wind blew across the beach. The amazing images persisted for at least 30 seconds and then disappeared.

The ghosts of Del Monte Beach most likely lost their lives in the surf or through boating accidents offshore, including shipboard fires or explosions and mysterious disappearances. The victims of numerous maritime disasters on Monterey Bay may gravitate to this beach, seeking dry land and help from the living.

For more than 150 years, Del Monte Beach has been a popular swimming site. At times, the surf runs high and creates dangerous, unseen undertows that catch weak swimmers and shallow-water waders by surprise. The last official total of deaths on or near this beach that I could find was a Monterey County document dated 1964. It reported 152 fatalities.

An associate who occasionally engages in paranormal investigations reported to me that he spotted the ghost of a young woman dressed in a Victorian-era bathing suit. While sitting on the beach under an overcast sky, he felt a presence next to him. He turned to see the nearly transparent figure sitting a few feet way. He told me later he nearly passed out when she spoke to him, asking, "Where am I?" A moment later, she vanished.

GHOSTS OF THE DEAD GUYS

La Casa Bodega Liquor and Deli
500 De Monte Avenue
Monterey 93940
831-655-3222

Reports can be found on the Internet about a robbery gone bad at this popular deli and liquor store. It has been reported that late one night in the 1970s two men entered the store intending to rob it. When the clerk failed to move fast enough, one of them pulled out a pistol and killed the man. The ghost of this unfortunate victim is said to appear near the cash register. Through a search of local newspaper archives, the state of California murder index, and interviews with the store's current owner, Otis Cribbs, and an employee, I was unable to corroborate this report. According to Otis, a man who operated a business in an adjacent building for nearly 50 years could not verify such as tragic event ever took place on the premises of La Casa Bodega. Nonetheless, I know two well-respected psychics who have independently discovered the spirit of a murder victim in this store.

Another ghost, derived from an accident, also shows up in the store. Before La Casa Bodega became a deli and liquor store, a man operated an auto repair shop in the building. Being an amateur scientist and inventor, the fellow designed and built a high-voltage device that created steam under high pressure. It is said this device blew up, killing the man instantly. Otis told me the fatal invention was designed to take the wrinkles out of fruit. Otis and his daughter have seen this ghost dressed in blue jeans and a white T-shirt. This spirit appears in the southwest corner of the deli, turns slowly as he takes in the new appearance of the place, and then vanishes. In contrast to his passive appearance, this ghost can be quite active. He has been known to knock items off shelves, move objects to irrational locations, and whisper garbled messages in the ears of employees and customers. Otis says, after closing the store late in the evening, the ghost sometimes yells "Hey" as the lights are turned off.

FLOATING CANDLES AND GHOSTLY BELLS

Royal Presidio Chapel
550 Church Street
Monterey 93940
831-373-4345

Early in the Spanish Period (1770-1820), a presidio was established in Monterey to protect Spain's most distant colony from intrusion by the English and Russians. Chapels or churches were always an integral part of Spanish military facilities throughout California. In Monterey, considerable resources were given to the construction of the chapel that still stands today. Built between 1791 and 1794, the chapel was erected on the site of three predecessors. These former structures were flimsy and made of wood and soft adobe; they were lost to fires and possibly earthquakes. With a design created at the Academy of San Carlos in Mexico City and stone construction, rather than adobe, the Royal Chapel has stood more than 200 years. The fine work of stonemason Manuel Ruiz and the skill of hundreds of Indian laborers have created a beautiful artifact of Spanish California, which captures the essence of the era without revealing its age.

The chapel has been designated "Royal" because the Spanish governor and other representatives of the King of Spain worshiped there. Late in the Mexican Period (1820-1846), the presidio and chapel fell into disrepair. It was saved from ruin in 1850 when it became the cathedral of the Bishop of Monterey. Its status as a cathedral, the smallest in the U.S., was renewed in 1968.

The Royal Chapel was the seat of religious devotion and social center for many residents of Monterey who lived half a world away from their homes and families in Europe. As such, the spirits of some of those early Californians still occupy the chapel. Staff and visitors have witnessed a bright candle moving in the darkness of the sanctuary, as if carried in the hand of an unseen being. The floating candle has been seen by two witnesses simultaneously in the choir loft, too.

Other ghostly activity includes the sound of sandal-clad feet walking down the aisle of the chapel, the swishing sound of long skirts moving through the pews, and the ringing of church bells in the middle of the night. When people rush to the bell tower to investigate the ringing, no explanation can be found. Local ghost hunters believe a Mexican servant who worked for the chapel priests remains to perform the honored duty left undone by the departed fathers.

Several reports suggest that not all the church's priests have left the place. In 1960, a priest reported that he heard a familiar speech arising from the darkness of the chapel. Turning on a few lights, he approached the still dim sanctuary and encountered the ghostly image of a priest conducting mass. This ghost even turned the pages of a large prayer book and lit candles. The astonished priest raced from

Built in 1771, the Royal Chapel of the Presidio of Monterey is one of the oldest buildings in California.

the church to the rectory to get someone to confirm the sighting, but when the two men returned, the ghost had vanished.

The ghost priest may be the apparition of a popular clergyman who served the church from 1890 to the early 1920s. Upon his retirement, he lived in the rectory for a few years before dying in 1930. The man's remains were transported to Los Angeles for burial in spite of his wishes to be interned in Monterey. During the ensuing 54 years, the priest's ghost appeared often on the rectory's second floor and elsewhere in the church. Dressed in priestly robes, this benevolent ghost has unnerved some witnesses; however, most of those who saw him were comforted by his presence. These sightings continued until 1984 when the priest's body was exhumed and reburied in Monterey.

Ghost activity in the rectory also has been attributed to other spirits. People working in the building in the evening have reported feeling touched by invisible hands and lights turning on and off. Some workers have reported an uneasy feeling, as if they are being watched by a being that does not want them in the building.

GHOST OF ROBERT LOUIS STEVENSON AND THE LADY IN BLACK

Robert Louis Stevenson House
530 Houston Street
Monterey 93940
831-649-7118

Named for the famous 19th-century author who lived here for only a year, the Robert Louis Stevenson House has been known to be haunted for more than 80 years. Built in the 1830s and operated as a boarding house and the French Hotel, the house has had countless visitors of some celebrity. American consul Thomas Larkin, Gen. Mariano Vallejo, Col. John C. Fremont, Commodore Sloat, and writer Richard Henry Dana spent time in the huge two-story adobe building, attending official government events, or socializing with members of Monterey's prominent families. By the 1870s, the edifice had been expanded to the large building that stands today as part of Monterey's State Historic Park.

In 1879, Robert Louis Stevenson rented rooms in the French Hotel and resided there with Fanny Osbourne, whom he later married in San Francisco. Although Robert was seriously ill most of the year, he still managed to spend time visiting with the lighthouse keeper Allen L. Luce, at Point Pinos Lighthouse, and write much of the classic story *Treasure Island.* Today, the Stevenson House contains one of the largest collections in the world of the family's memorabilia and artifacts. These personal items and Stevenson's experiences, including his illness, may account for the ghostly activity in the house, some of which is attributed to Stevenson.

Several visitors and docents have reported hearing a muted cough on the second floor, thinking someone had suddenly become sick. It is known that Stevenson suffered from tuberculosis and was plagued with an incessant cough. In conjunction with these sounds, the odor of carbolic acid, used to disinfect rooms of the sick, has also been detected on the second floor in a room once occupied by Stevenson.

Other unexplained audio phenomena include the sound of a heavy trunk being dragged across the wood plank floor of the second story. Rushing to that floor, docents found that Stevenson's old trunk had been moved into the hallway. In a nearby room used as study, several of Stevenson's books have been found pulled from the shelves and opened to well-worn pages.

No one has reported encounters with Stevenson's apparition, but psychics and ghost hunters who have toured the house have reported bizarre experiences that suggest strong remnants from the 19th century are present at various locations. Looking in a mirror, these visitors have reported seeing visions of the house as it appears in the 1870s, complete with furniture, curtains, paintings hung on the walls no longer on display, and people moving about.

The most active ghost in the Stevenson House may be that of owner Manuela Girardin. In 1879, this unfortunate woman lost her husband and spent several weeks nursing her two grandchildren while they suffered from a life-threatening fever. Though the children survived, Manuela's experience created some intense environmental imprints that have been detected by countless visitors and guides.

The ghost of Fanny Osbourne may be the famous Lady in Black who haunts this historic house. The ghost of Robert Louis Stevenson may be there, too.

Many people have reported seeing an elderly woman on the second floor. Dressed in a long, black, old-fashioned Spanish gown, she walks the hallway and appears in the nursery. Her lifelike apparition has been seen sitting on the children's bed or standing nearby. Some have noticed a worried expression on her face. One visitor spoke to the woman, thinking she was a costumed docent. The apparition replied in Spanish and then vanished. In the nursery, toys and furniture have been seen moving about by invisible hands. The smell of roses has been detected there, too. Unexplained cold spots are routinely encountered in each of the rooms and the hallway of the second floor.

There may be several other ghosts in the Stevenson House. Passersby on the street and people milling about in the garden have heard blood-curdling screams. It has been reported that a resident of the house once endured the amputation of his leg after a terrible accident. The emotional imprint of the surgery, performed with nothing more than rum as an anesthetic, remains as a terrifying scream.

On the back stairs, the apparition of a dark-haired woman dressed in a white dress appears with variable strength. At times, the spirit is completely transparent and partial while some witnesses have reported that she appears completely lifelike. Reports indicate that a saddle maker who lived in the house murdered her on the back stairs. Audio phenomena detected at the site consist of the voices of a man and woman in a heated argument, which has led to speculation that the man killed the young woman when she demanded he leave her alone.

The ghosts of a well-dressed man and woman walking arm in arm toward the house have been seen in the backyard. In addition, a gardener once reported that, while working on his hands and knees, he noticed a pair of shoes topped with green pants nearby. Thinking he had a visitor interested in the garden, the man looked up but saw nothing above the apparition's knees.

GHOST OF THE FAMOUS FAMILY

Casa Munras Hotel and Spa
700 Munras Avenue
Monterey 93940
800-222-2446
www.hotelcasamunras.com

The beautiful Casa Munras Hotel and Spa offers all the amenities modern travelers expect in this hacienda-inspired setting. Its sun-washed white and ochre walls, beamed ceilings, terra cotta patios, tile roofs, and covered verandas comprise a charming display of colonial Spanish architecture, which blends well with the relaxed atmosphere of Monterey. Few visitors and guests of the hotel realize the hotel's central portion dates from the 1820s. Constructed by Esteban Carlos Munras, the hacienda was the first to be established outside the walls of the old Spanish presidio. Munras's decision to erect his grand house beyond the safety of presidio walls represents a turning point in Monterey's evolution from a military outpost to a city. The old, historic structure has been meticulously restored and maintained, blending with newer construction to produce the world-class Casa Munras Hotel and Spa.

Born in 1798, Esteban Munras arrived in Monterey about 1819 from his native Barcelona, Spain. Some historical accounts identify him as a trader, but his first job in Monterey was as a fresco painter. In 1820, Munras was hired by Father Juan Cabot to create murals in the Mission San Miguel de Arcángel near Paso Robles. These beautiful neoclassical murals still exist at the mission as a testament to Munras's great skill as an artist. With the support of mission fathers, Munras applied for a land grant and received several thousand acres on which he established cattle herds. With this resource, he entered the hide and tallow trade meticulously described in Richard Henry Dana's book *Two Years Before the Mast*. The wealth generated by this business supported the construction of the *grande* hacienda and the creation of a large family.

Don Estaban died in Monterey in 1850, but his ghost still roams the hallways of his historic home. He gives the impression that he is pleased with the hotel and the people who now visit it. There is no frightening or destructive paranormal activity here. Munras creates intense cold spots, operates coffee makers, flicks lights on and off, calls staff members by name, and gives sensitive people the distinct impression they are being shadowed by a strong male presence.

When I toured the Munras hacienda with ghost tour guide Gary Munsinger, we searched for a female ghost believed to be the daughter of Don Esteban. Dona Esteban Munras Catalina Manzanelli Ponce de Leon, a descendent of the famous explorer, lived at the hacienda for many years and died in one of its rooms. Her apparition has been spotted in the second-floor hallways. She appears as a short, thin woman dressed in a long, black Spanish gown with a long lace shawl falling from her shoulders and a mantilla in her hair. Sightings of her apparition are rare, but staff and visitors often hear the rustle of a gown as she glides through the hallways.

THE PARTY GHOSTS

Stokes Restaurant and Bar
500 Hartnell Street
Monterey 93940
831-373-1110
www.stokesrestaurant.com

The large adobe housing the popular Stokes Restaurant and Bar was constructed in 1833 by Hoge and Benjamin Day. Renovations and several additions throughout the years have enlarged the structure while preserving the classic Mexican colonial style. It stands today amid a grove of trees in what was once the heart of old Monterey. The modern restaurant and crowds of patrons don't detract from the 19th-century ambiance nor have they driven away the many ghosts that haunt the place.

Arriving in Monterey in 1834, English sailor James Stokes immediately saw fantastic possibilities for a better life. Snatching the ship's medicine cases and the navigator's fancy coat, he jumped ship and landed in town, introducing himself as Dr. James Stokes. In a

Built in 1833, the Stokes Restaurant has been the scene of numerous ghost sightings linked to deaths that occurred in the 19th century.

small adobe, he opened a pharmacy and began treating the town's people. According to Monterey Ghost Tours guide Gary Munsinger, many of Stokes's patients died under his care. The high death rate didn't detract from his reputation, however. Stokes eventually became the personal physician of Mexican governor Jose Figueroa. In less than a year, the governor was dead, but Stokes's medical business continued to thrive.

By 1837, Stokes had enough money to buy the house constructed by the Days. With his social standing and fortune growing, he married a widow, Josefa Sota de Cano, and moved her and her four children into his house. A few years later, James and Josefa had two children of their own. To accommodate the large family, Stokes added a second floor to the house and a ground floor wing for a large kitchen. Apparently, fewer numbers of Stokes's patients were dying during this period because his home became the social center of the town, hosting the annual Cascaron Ball, which is still staged in Monterey today. In addition, Stokes became mayor.

The Stokeses outwardly happy life came to an end in 1855 when

Josefa died in the upstairs bedroom. The death must have caused Stokes to go insane because he was caught in the act of violating his daughter that same night. Pulled from the bed by his two sons, Stokes grabbed a bottle of poison, swallowed its contents, and died on the floor of the room.

This tragic story of a natural death followed by a suicide suggests Stokes's household was not the peaceful, happy place one might expect. In fact, something has kept the spirit of James and Josefa in the house more than a century after their deaths.

In Josefa's bedroom, now a second-floor dining room, a variety of bizarre sounds have been heard, including the voices of several women engaged in an animated conversation, an infant crying, footsteps, slamming doors, and the breaking of several bottles as they hit floor. When the owners or staff investigate, no explanation can be found. On one occasion, after closing for the night, two workers heard a loud crash from the second floor, as if a china cabinet had tipped over. Rushing to the site of the commotion, they found nothing out of place.

On the first floor, several staff members have been tapped on the shoulder, pushed, and even shaken by strong hands. It is believed this is the ghostly activity of Dr. Stokes. In the restaurant, this ghost has rearranged table settings and caused a large candelabrum to slide across the piano in front of several astonished witnesses.

The apparition of an elderly woman dressed in an ankle-length skirt has been spotted standing in the loft overlooking the bar. This apparition also appears on the stairs and on the street in front of the restaurant.

Aside from James and Josefa, many people believe the ghost of a later resident, Hattie Gragg, haunts the Stokes Restaurant and Bar. In 1890, Mortimer and Martha Harriet "Hattie" Gragg purchased the old adobe and continued the Stokes's tradition of staging the town's most important social events in their home. Since her death in 1948, much of the paranormal activity in the house has been attributed to Hattie. Her ghost has been seen on the stairs and in the bar and accused of flicking the lights on and off, playing the piano, moving wine glasses, and calling out the names of restaurant employees. The din of female conversation heard on the second floor may be Hattie and her friends gossiping during one of the grand parties she held in her home.

COLTON HALL AND JAIL

Pacific Street at Madison
Monterey 93940
831-646-5640
www.historicmonterey.org/?p=colton_hall

Constructed in the late 1840s by Rev. Walter Colton, this grand hall was the first government building erected after the American annexation of Alta California from Mexico in June of 1846. Rooms on the first floor housed a school and offices, and the 70-by-30-foot hall on the second floor was used for public assemblies. The most important assembly to take place was the constitutional convention of 1849, during which a state government was formed and an application for admission to the Union was signed by delegates from all over the Territory of California. In later years, Colton Hall served as a public school, county courthouse, sheriff's office, and Monterey city police headquarters. Today, it is fully restored to its 1849 appearance and open as a museum. The second-floor meeting hall contains desks, writing implements, and reproductions of historic maps and other documents that were perused by delegates during the constitutional convention. Behind the building stands the town's jail, used from 1851 to 1939. The jail is also open to the public as a museum.

Is Colton Hall haunted? The many docents who have worked there over the years have reported so many strange experiences that there is no other reasonable explanation than to except that ghosts are all over the place. The second floor of the portico was used as a gallows, where such criminals as the infamous Anastacio Garcia were disposed of. Garcia was convicted of murdering two Monterey men. While awaiting his court-appointed execution date, vigilantes stormed the jail, knocked the guard to the ground (in a painless gesture designed to protect the man's dignity and his job), pulled Garcia from his cell, and hanged him from the portico balcony. It may be his ghost or the

In 1849, California's constitutional convention convened in Colton Hall. Later, its balcony was used as a gallows.

This jail sits behind Colton Hall. Several of the region's notorious outlaws were housed there, including Anastascio Garcia.

ghosts of others who were hanged creating the intense cold spots on the balcony. Guides and visitors have also reported the eerie sensation of being watched, taps on the shoulder, and disembodied footsteps. Sensitives visiting the second-floor assembly hall have heard bursts of sound resembling several men talking simultaneously. This may be a remnant of one of the spirited debates that occurred during the 1849 convention.

While visiting the jail, my son, Michael, and I heard a bizarre voice directed at us from one of the unoccupied and locked, cells. After shooting a few pictures through the bars of the cell door, we turned away but stopped when we heard, "Hey, hey, hey?" in a rough, male voice come from the cell. The pictures did not capture orbs, but, suddenly, we smelled a foul odor at the cell door. Perhaps a ghostly prisoner had noticed us and rushed to the door seeking help.

GHOST OF THE OLD BANDITO

Vasquez Adobe
546 Dutra Street
Monterey 93440

City employees who work in this building often experience the ghostly activities of spirits who may be related to the Old Bandito, Tiburcio Vasquez. The paranormal activity may originate from the bad guy, himself. Ghost tours operator Gary Munsinger tells his guests about Tiburcio, but he reminds them that other ghosts are present in the aged building.

The Vasquez Adobe was constructed in 1832 by Luis Placencia and immediately purchased by Guadalupe Cantua de Vasquez. Her son Tiburcio was born in the house in 1835 and lived there until he began his life of crime in 1849. At the age of 14, he stabbed a

In the 1840s, the infamous bandit Tiburcio Vasquez used this house as a hideout from sheriff's deputies. Once owned by Vasquez's sister, the building now houses city offices.

deputy sheriff and then embarked on a crime spree that would last until 1874 when he was hanged for multiple murders, rape, and robberies from San Benito County to Los Angeles. Short periods of incarceration, including a few years in San Quentin, did not cool his blood. Inflamed by his sensitivity to racial injustice and intense desire for revenge against Americans who he considered interlopers in Alta California, Vasquez became known as the second most murderous criminal in the state behind the notorious Joaquin Murrieta.

Each time Vasquez escaped from jail or earned a release, he returned to his mother's house in Monterey. Blending in with the largely Hispanic population, he enjoyed a few months of rest before rumors spread of his presence and he was chased out of town.

Vasquez's ghost may be generating the ghostly activity in the old Vasquez Adobe. In death, he may have returned to the only place in California where he found respite from eager lawmen, posses, and bounty hunters.

The building is now used as offices for city employees. Many workers have reported strange occurrences—telephone lights flashing, indicating someone is making a call when all phones are off; unexplained foot steps on the second floor when it is known no one is working on that floor; intense cold spots; amorphous shadows that cannot be explained; objects disappearing and then reappearing in unexpected places; and disquieting sensations of an unseen entity.

In the 1960s, students at the Hopkins Marine Station were housed here. Years later, some of them reported that they often heard the loud foot falls of heavy boots on the second story's wood floor. On some occasions, the sound was so loud that students ran to the two staircases hoping to catch a burglar, but no living being was seen.

Access to the building is limited, but visitors walking the verandas at night have observed strange lights moving around inside the building. EVP recorded there have included noises described as "knocking" or "thumping."

THE INFANT SPIRIT

Lara-Soto Adobe
460 Pierce Street
Monterey 93940

One of the hot spots visited by Gary Munsinger's popular Monterey Ghost Tours is the charming Lara-Soto Adobe. Although the land was granted to Dona Feliciana Lara in 1849, a crude house may have stood on the property since the early 1830s. The Lara-Soto Adobe stood vacant from 1860 to 1897 and was restored in the 1920s. John Steinbeck bought the home in October of 1944. He and his wife, Gwyn, and infant son, Thom, lived there for a year while the Noble-prize winning author wrote the novel *The Pearl*. It is said that Steinbeck had the house exorcised before he moved in. It is likely that

Built in the 1840s, the Lara-Soto adobe was the scene of a tragic death long before author John Steinbeck moved in.

he heard the rumors that still circulate around Monterey about the property being haunted by the ghost of a three-year-old boy who died there.

The huge Monterey cypress, which stands so close to the house that its roots lift some of the porch tiles, marks the child's grave. Horticulturalists believe the tree was planted in the 1830s, prior to the construction of the Lara-Soto Adobe. Legend says the parents of the dead child planted the seedling on the grave as a marker that would stand for centuries.

In the 1980s, excavation of the ground around the tree was performed to improve drainage of the property. There are unconfirmed reports that workers uncovered the bones of a child. Rather than exhume the remains and perform an archeological evaluation of the site, the property's owner left the bones in place and restored the ground.

Today, visitors to the porch of the Lara-Soto Adobe take photographs in search of orbs. Others attempt to use psychic sensitivities to experience remnants of the death. It is likely the family of the dead child spent many hours, for many years, at this gravesite since it is located at the end of the porch. Frequent, intense, repetitive emotions have created imprints that are still strong enough to be detected.

GHOST OF JACK SWAN

California's First Theater
Pacific Avenue at Scott Street
Monterey 93940
831-649-7118

In the early 1840s, Jack Swan sailed into Monterey Bay aboard an English merchant ship. Being a sailor before the mast (a low-ranking sailor), he probably thought Monterey was the most beautiful place he had ever seen. The blue water of the bay and white-sand beaches were enticing enough, but the charming town with its sun-baked adobe buildings capped with red tile roofs and lush gardens were probably overwhelming attractions for a man who had spent years at sea, eating bad food and living in squalor with twenty other men in a

Jack Swan constructed this building in 1844 to house California's first theater. He and actors haunt the stage and bar.

ship's forecastle. Within days of his arrival, he had signed off the ship's manifest, taken his pay in gold, and purchased a lot with a view of the harbor. With frequent thanks to his lucky stars, Jack Swan lived a long and prosperous life in Monterey. He died in 1896 and was buried in Cementerio el Encinal on Fremont Street. His remains may be dust, but his spirit still manages the bar and theater he established in his adobe on Pacific Avenue.

When Jack opened his business in 1844, it was intended to be a boarding house and bar for sailors. Soon after the American annexation of Alta California in 1846, the building became a theater. Soldiers from Colonel Stevenson's regiment, the First New York Volunteer, stationed in Monterey, wished to stage a play to alleviate their boredom. Since Swan had one of the largest rooms in town, they prevailed upon him to let them construct a small stage and perform the play *Putnam, the Iron Son of '76* for their shipmates. Anticipating large profits from the admission fee and drinks ordered from the bar, Jack agreed. Apparently, the event brought in a lot of money; the place was kept in continuous use as a theater until 1937, long after Jack had passed away. However, his death has not kept him from managing the place.

People who have worked in the building for decades have passed on stories of ghostly activity. One employee reported several experiences to local writer Randall Reinstedt. Over a period of more than 25 years, she observed objects moving about, things disappearing and then reappearing at other locations near the stage, unexplainable noises, and sightings of Jack Swan's apparition. During rehearsals, actors who forgot their lines have heard a strange voice whisper the words in their ears, and theater workers have heard Jack's voice emanating from the costume closet. It is said that when he speaks, the air feels electrically charged. Ghost hunters might want to explore this place with an EMF meter and audio recorder for EVP.

I've seen the ghost of Jack Swan on three occasions. My first encounter, in the early 1980s, was early in the afternoon when no other visitors were in the building. From the rear of the theater, I spotted a short, thin man sitting on the edge of the stage. His upper body appeared lifelike, but his legs, clothed in black pants, seemed transparent. As I approached the man, I could see he had long, thin white hair that was almost glowing. He also had a long white beard. As I stepped closer, less than ten feet away, he vanished.

The next day, I returned to the theater to search for the ghost. I found him standing next to the bar with a wide grin on his face. Again, as I approached him, he faded from view. An intense cold spot was left where the apparition had stood.

In 2008, with my son, Michael, I passed by the theater on a cold, moonless night. As we walked, complaining about the cold wind, we heard a loud crash and the bottles coming together from the theater. Looking through separate windows, we both saw the apparition of a short, bearded man scurrying between the bar and the theater. He made three passes, back and forth, before he disappeared.

Security guards have also reported encounters with the ghost of Jack Swan. One of them found a white flower on the hood of his car after spotting a pale apparition of a bearded man crossing the street. At the time, the only source of white flowers in the neighborhood was a shrub in the theater's backyard.

GHOST OF THE MURDERER

Perry-Downer House
201 Van Buren Street
Monterey 93940
831-375-9182

Activity of the ghost that haunts this unique 18th-century house illustrates the attachment of a spirit to the place of death. However, the story is not about the victim. It is about the murderer.

The wood-frame Victorian house was built in 1860 by whaling ship captain Manuel Perry. Perched on a hill high above old Monterey, the home offered a grand view of the bay and provided a geographic separation from the bars and brothels visited by rowdy sailors who landed in town after months at sea. Captain Perry built the house in a style reminiscent of New England homes to ease whatever stress his wife, Mary de Mello Silva, might have felt after relocating from her home in Boston.

Descendants of the Perry family remodeled the house in 1910 by elevating the single-story home and adding a new ground floor. By the 1920s, the place had been sold and opened as a boarding house. One of the borders was a popular young woman who enjoyed spending evenings away from her jealous boyfriend, socializing with men who were passing through Monterey. One night, while the woman was dressing for the evening, the boyfriend stormed through the front door of the house, raced up the stairs, and stopped her from leaving her room. In a jealous rage, the man strangled her.

In 1966, after major renovations by Webster and Marguerite Downer, stories of bizarre experiences began to circulate around Monterey. In one of the second-floor bedrooms, doors slam shut and a suffocating atmosphere overwhelms some visitors. One person reported that she felt an unseen entity chase her from the room and down the stairs.

When paranormal experts began looking into this story, they anticipated finding a female ghost. Instead, the ghost they encountered was male and quite belligerent. Apparently, this fellow doesn't want anyone investigating the scene of his crime. Still seething with jealous

The wood-framed Perry-Downer house is haunted by a ghost who may have committed a murder in the 1920s.

rage, and unaware of his death, he may be waiting for his girlfriend to return to the room.

There may be other ghosts in this charming house. A historic costume collection maintained by the Monterey History and Art Association may have a few spirits attached to 18th-century dresses and suits donated by many of the region's oldest families.

TREASURE, GRAVES, AND GHOSTS

Monterey Custom House
20 Custom House Plaza
Monterey 93940
831-649-7118

Built of adobe in 1821, the stately Mexican Custom House sits at the foot of Fisherman's Wharf overlooking the former anchorage for sailing ships from Spain, Portugal, England, Mexico, and the

The Spanish Custom House is a Monterey landmark that may be haunted by ghosts guarding a buried treasure.

American East Coast. After the arduous passage around Cape Horn, many ships arrived in need of repairs and with crews decimated by illness. To ship captains and exhausted crews, dropping anchor in the still waters of Monterey was a sign of salvation. To citizens of Monterey, the arrival of ships was a great event. Cargoes of clothing, furniture, machinery, medicine, newspapers, and mail were eagerly awaited and vital to the welfare of the community. All of these items were hauled ashore, inspected, and taxed at the Custom House before merchants could move them to their stores for sale. Often, valuable goods were sold to excited customers as wagons rolled away from the Custom House.

The Custom House continued to serve as the hub of commerce in California until 1860. Throughout the remainder of the 19th century and the first decades of the 20th century, the place was rented to various entrepreneurs for use as a warehouse, store, meeting hall, or residence. The residents of the place, whose names are lost to history, could be the basis of reports of ghostly activity.

Among the clamor reported by visitors are footsteps, deafening rattles, wishing sounds emanating from the thick adobe walls, and creaking doors. In addition, several intense cold spots tend to move from room to room.

Apparitions include a Mexican man and a boy who have conveyed, through psychics, that they were murdered in the building. The man has complained to living persons that he was killed for his gold and buried, with the boy who was also murdered, near the stairs leading to the tower. Excavation of the spot did not uncover graves or treasure, but it is possible the bodies were placed elsewhere under the floor or later moved by criminals to avoid prosecution for murder. Locals believe this man still haunts the Custom House, awaiting the help of someone who would find his grave and give him a proper burial.

Over the past 50 years, reports have surfaced in the local newspaper and magazines about ghosts trying to rid the place of residents. In the 1930s, a resident claimed he was tossed out of bed three times in one night by spirits who did not want him there. Some ghosts express their displeasure with tourists by creating areas or cells of cold air or thick atmosphere that lend a sense of foreboding.

The Custom House may be occupied by several other lost souls who died thousands of miles from home in a country that was, at the time, on the other side of the world. At various times, the buildings served as a clinic for sick seamen and Monterey's citizens during epidemics. Today, the Custom House is a popular tourist destination. It is also a good place to hunt for ghosts, especially in the morning before sightseers arrive. I've visited the place more than 30 times and encountered paranormal phenomena during most of those visits. Typically, I find intense cold spots close to the stairs. As a psychic investigator, I've detected numerous voices speaking in Spanish, the sound of boots treading the floorboards, and isolated spots blanketed in dread and fear.

Archeological excavations performed in 1991 discovered foundations of structures predating the Custom House. In fact, there may have been at least two previous structures erected by the Spanish military to protect the harbor. I have contacted a number of people involved in the excavations and inquired about valuables that might have been found. On every occasion, I was told that no information was available about gold coins or currency that may have been discovered at the site.

I encountered the same story when I researched rumors of treasure at the Blue Wing Inn Sonoma.

GHOST OF FRED AND OTHER SPIRITS

Monterey Hotel
406 Alvarado Street
Monterey 93940

Hardly making an appearance on the radar screens of many of the region's ghost hunters, the Monterey Hotel, I've discovered, is a hot spot for paranormal activity, complete with disembodied voices, moving objects, spirit manipulation of electronic devices, creepy atmospheric changes signaling a ghostly presence, and apparitions.

The Monterey Hotel's turn-of-the-century sculpted façade overlooks busy Alvarado Street, presenting a fascinating face not readily spotted

The Monterey Hotel is haunted by several ghosts who add to the charm of this 1904 landmark.

by the hordes of tourists roaming the waterfront just two blocks away. To ghost hunters who know what to look for, the exterior of the hotel boldly proclaims there is something different about the place. Ornate moldings, bay windows, decorative masonry oak leaves, and some amazing brick work, capped with a large medallion engraved with the year of the hotel's construction, 1904, reveal enticing glimpses of a long-past era. These amazing architectural features, in contrast to the Spanish and Mexican architecture for which Monterey is known, arouse strong suspicions that spirits of some of the people who once lived or worked in the building are still there. Indeed, based on the reports of staff and guests of the Monterey Hotel and my personal experiences during an overnight stay, there is no doubt the place is haunted.

The four-story hotel was constructed in 1904 at a cost of $100,000. Seventy guest rooms were served by a single elevator and about 30 bathrooms. The ornate elevator cage, with gilt edging and fancy beveled glass, is still in place but not operational. For decades, the hotel was one of the most popular and successful on the Monterey peninsula. By 1960, however, guest arrivals had dropped off and the place was run down. Renovations costing millions of dollars were done in 1982 and again in 1996. Hand-carved stair railings and posts, redwood ceilings, ornate crown moldings, doorway surrounds, and numerous other architectural features were meticulously restored, re-creating the hotel's original European style. These spectacular early-20th-century features, together with antique reproduction mirrors and furniture on every floor, create an atmosphere that is entirely different from nearby Spanish and Mexican buildings.

In January of 2009, I had the opportunity to interview staff and talk to Maureen Doran, vice president of Moonstone Properties, the company that owns the hotel. She made available to me the hotel's most haunted room, suite 217. In this room, my son and I heard the two TVs and a clock radio emit a loud "pop," usually three times in rapid succession, sounding like a high-voltage electrical device arcing. This gave me the impression that some unseen entity was trying to communicate.

In the early morning, while moving about my suite, I heard a clear, incorporeal male voice talk for several minutes about "75 stairs." He kept saying "going up" and "coming down" and "gotta fix 75 stairs." He sounded tired when he talked about "fixing the carpet on 75 stairs." A short time later, I learned a hotel maintenance man died on the premises, perhaps on the stairs or by an accident that occurred in the antique elevator. Staff members have named this ghost Fred. The number 75 must be significant to this ghost. At one time during my stay, he filled the screen of my son's cell phone with repeating digits, 7 and 5.

Staff members told me about the ghost image of a girl who appeared to be about 13 years old. This girl has been spotted sitting on the stairs adjacent to the front desk, scaring the night clerk into a sweat. Guests have encountered this ghost upstairs. One man, who happened to be a sensitive and a medium, was so bothered by the girl's presence and constant talking that he declined to spend his wedding night in the elegant hotel.

The image of a man dressed in Edwardian clothing, complete with high hat, has been seen in the mirror facing the front desk. The mirror is a reproduction, not an antique, but this ghost uses it to makes his appearances. I suspect this is the spirit of the building's architect; William Henry Weeks, who died in 1936. Mr. Weeks designed several buildings that still stand near the Monterey Hotel.

The hotel is also a hot spot for EVP enthusiasts. I recorded a loud, clear "Hello" when I asked for any communication from spirits on the second floor. Several staff members have felt the disembodied touch of cold hands, heard voices whispering in their ears, found objects moved to bizarre locations, and witnessed doors moving without explanation.

If you plan to visit the Monterey peninsula, I recommend the Monterey Hotel. Located in the heart of the old town close to several historic, and haunted, Spanish and Mexican buildings, the hotel is a perfect base from which to stage ghost hunting adventures in old Monterey.

DOC RICKETTS' DEATH SITE

Wave Street at Drake Avenue, at Cannery Row's east end, intersection
   with the bike path
Monterey 93940

On May 8, 1948, Ed "Doc" Ricketts (1897-1948), a marine biologist, drove his battered, old Buick out of the garage under his lab and headed down Cannery Row toward central Monterey. It was after 5:00 P.M., and Ed was hungry for a steak dinner. As he drove down the street, his mind wandered to the many pressing problems he faced. Changes in the local fishing industry and difficulties keeping his laboratory going were worrying him. As Wave Street curved to the right, he turned his big Buick and pressed on the accelerator a little more. The engine responded with more power and more noise, enough to obscure the sound of the approaching Del Monte Express.

Based on eyewitness accounts, Ed never saw the train. Traveling at 30 to 40 miles per hour, the train slammed into the driver's side of Ed's car, crushing it. The impact didn't immediately kill him. A huge crowd of Cannery Row residents gathered at the scene and watched as firefighters took nearly an hour to extricate Ed from the crushed vehicle. He was taken to a local hospital where he lingered for 72 hours before "giving up the ghost." During that time, he regained consciousness only once and asked, "Is it bad?"

Everyone on Cannery Row was devastated by Ed Ricketts' death. He had been such a prominent character on the Row that his passing signaled the end of an era, one that had been celebrated in John Steinbeck's books *Cannery Row* (1945) and *Sweet Thursday* (1954). Ed, the original party animal and lady's man, was kind to everyone and always generous with his beer and money. Doc, as his friends and acquaintances knew him, was the heart and soul of Cannery Row.

Just as everyone loved Doc, Doc loved the Row. Many fans of Steinbeck's books have become fans of Doc. These followers leave flowers and other offerings around the statue that marks the site of Doc's fatal accident. Others hold vigils late at night, savoring the essence of the hour as they try to tune into the old days on the Row. The anniversary of Doc's tragic accident is an important time for getting in touch with the spirit of the neighborhood and the spirit of Doc Ricketts.

Many sensitives who have visited the site have detected the huge outpouring of emotion that took place on May 8 when nearby residents surrounded the wreckage and prayed Doc would survive. EVP captured here contain the sounds of sobbing, a female voice humming, a train, and grinding metal. Several people have reported unexplained cold spots around the site that follow the path taken by the train.

The old railroad right-of-way is now a bike path, but the former roadway traveled by the Del Monte Express is clearly marked with two lengths of the steel track imbedded in concrete. Doc's statue is near the scene.

DOC RICKETTS' LAB

800 Cannery Row
Monterey 943940
831-372-8512 (Cannery Row Foundation)

A short distance down the street from the world-famous Monterey Bay Aquarium sits a squatty, weathered, wooden building with a narrow, warped staircase. John Steinbeck made this building famous as the lab of marine biologist Edward "Doc" Ricketts and the central

Doc Ricketts' lab on Cannery Row was the scene of wild parties and frequent visits by author John Steinbeck.

venue in his 1945 classic *Cannery Row*. The forlorn lab sits among larger reconstructed buildings on revitalized Cannery Row. In the days of Steinbeck and Ricketts, the lab was the scene of many afternoons spent in philosophical discourse, lubricated with beer from Wing Chong Grocery across the street. After sundown, it was the place for all-night drinking sessions and riotous parties that often included Monterey police.

In 1957, the lab was purchased by 14 local businessmen, many of whom had been close friends of Doc and Steinbeck. They preserved the famous lab, keeping the interior untouched from the day Doc died in May 1948. In 1993, with exclusive membership declining, the building was sold to the city of Monterey. Today, access is extremely limited. The lab is open to the public only three times each year: John Steinbeck's birthday, February 27; Doc Rickett's birthday, May 14; and during the Sardine Festival, early June. On the remaining days of the year, fans of Steinbeck and Ricketts climb the narrow steps and sit for a while, pondering the wild parties and unique lives that gave the lab immortality.

Some people who sit upon those hallowed steps are there hoping to glimpse a ghost. Strange glowing lights have been observed moving up and down the steps and hovering over the tiny porch. Bizarre EVP, including scratching noises, howls, and hisses, have been captured there, too. I have not found any credible reports of apparitions aside from my own observations made in October of 1988. While roaming the Row late at night, I stopped across the street from the lab and watched the place for a while. The normally busy street was quiet. A heavy rain had fallen earlier that evening, driving tourists back to their hotel rooms. After studying the details of the weathered, wooden building draped with shadows created by the dim glow of streetlights, I heard the sound of creaking hinges and groaning wood as if the front door had opened. Noticing the door was shut, I focused on the porch and spotted a dark humanoid form turn from the door and descend the stairs. This apparition had few details, but I could see it moved with the gait of an energetic man, almost hopping down the steps. The image vanished before reaching the street. I rushed across the street and began an EVP sweep; my recorder did not capture anything.

I have since visited the lab more than 20 times but never again spotted that intriguing apparition. As for its identity, it could be anyone. I'd like to think it was Doc or Steinbeck, but, as Steinbeck's book explains, the lab was the heart and soul of Cannery Row and any number of spirits could be attached to it for myriad reasons.

There are several reports of apparitions in the vicinity of the lab. These "street ghosts" usually appear dressed as fishermen or cannery workers. They've been spotted on David, Irving, and Prescott avenues, always walking uphill as if they are heading home after a hard day of sardine fishing or work in the steaming canneries. Astonished witnesses describe these full-bodied and detailed apparitions as ghostly, with hollow eyes and stern expressions. Some of them attract the attention of witnesses because they stagger while others appear to float up the street before they vanish.

WING CHONG GROCERY

835 Cannery Row
Monterey 93940

Opened in 1918, this Cannery Row building once housed Wing Chong Grocery made famous by John Steinbeck in the books *Cannery Row* and *Sweet Thursday*. In his works of fiction that may be closer to the truth than any academic history of Cannery Row, Steinbeck changed the name of the owner, Won Yee, to Lee Chong, possibly as a gesture toward protecting the man's privacy. If that was the author's motive, it didn't work. Grocer Won Yee, who later became known as Wing Chong, has, in a literary sense, become internationally known and immortal. Nearly 60 years after the store faded into the blur of the Row's economic disintegration in the early 1950s, the place has become a kind of mecca or shrine for Steinbeck fans who visit it seeking some spiritual connection with the Nobel Prize-winning author or characters such as Doc Ricketts who visited the store daily to purchase beer.

Over the years, various businesses have occupied the building, offering the usual tourist souvenirs of T-shirts, key-chains, plastic sharks and squids, guidebooks, and other junk that might serve as evidence of a visit to the famous Row, but none of that has dissipated the essence of the grocery described by Steinbeck. The place was "not a model of neatness, but a miracle of supply." Aside from the vast array of groceries, Wing Chong offered everything a person might need, from cigars and whiskey to silk kimonos and fishing gear.

Visitors have looked for the ghost of the venerable, wise businessman, Won Yee, or Lee Chong, but there is little evidence that his spirit haunts his workplace. The ghost that is most active in the old grocery is believed to be that of a young man. His name is unknown, but locals who are familiar with the history of the building, and businesses that have occupied it, believe he was a dishwasher for a small café that once occupied part of the ground floor. This fellow was murdered at a young age. His body was found on the railroad tracks behind the building.

Witnesses report that the saloon-style double doors at the rear of the store swing open as if an invisible entity had dashed through them, heading to the front of the store. This ghost moves with such energy that a witness standing nearby and holding a newspaper noticed the pages shake. Moments later, the doors swung open again as the ghost retraced his steps to the back room of the building. This ghostly activity has been witnessed by two people simultaneously. At times, the spirit shows up for work with great regularity, bursting through the doors precisely at 3:00 P.M.

GHOSTS OF THE CANNERY WORKERS

Monterey Bay Aquarium
866 Cannery Row
Monterey 93940
831-648-4800
www.montereybayaquarium.com

The world-famous Monterey Bay Aquarium is usually filled with visitors who wander from one building to the next, amazed at the vast collection of marine life held in unbelievably huge tanks of seawater. Many people who take the time to look at the exterior and interior architectural features assume the entire structure, built in the early 1980s, is merely a facsimile of the old canneries that once filled Cannery Row. Like Disneyland, the place resembles a re-creation of the historic street and preserves, in some ways, the quaint atmosphere of the 1930s when sardines were the cash crop of Monterey Bay. Few people realize that a large portion of the aquarium sits on the site of the old Hovden Cannery, which was among the first to open on Cannery Row and the last to close in the 1960s. In fact, the exterior walls of the Hovden Cannery were saved from demolition and incorporated into the new structure, where offices, labs, and other facilities are located.

The incorporation of the original cannery into the new aquarium may be the basis of reported hauntings. Employees have been surprised to find strangely dressed people in the facility after closing. One apparition, a female, was described by a flustered employee as short and wearing a white dress covered with a heavy apron, a hair net, and gloves. This apparition has been seen many times in various locations throughout the Hovden portion of the aquarium. When employees ask if the lady needs help, she usually does not respond and simply vanishes. Occasionally, she replies in a language that sounds like Portuguese. The ghostly cannery worker shows up most frequently in the entry area near the preserved brick ovens.

In one of the newest portions of the sprawling aquarium, the unseen ghost of a man taps tourists on the shoulder. At the entrance

The world-famous Monterey Bay Aquarium includes architectural elements from the old Hovden fish cannery that once occupied the site. The entrance to the outer banks exhibit may be a vortex.

to the Outer Banks exhibit, visitors pass through a circular space surrounded, above head level, by a unique fish tank filled with sardines. A machine-generated current keeps the water circulating counterclockwise and the huge school of fish swims into it, moving slowly ahead, circumnavigating the tank every five to ten minutes. Some people stand in the center of the space mesmerized by movement of the shiny fish, or some unseen electromagnetic field created by the rapid movement of seawater. Many who stand at this location feel an unseen being tap them on the shoulder and whisper something in their ear. When words are heard, the language is identified as Spanish or Portuguese. No further identifying information has been reported. It is most likely the ghost is a former cannery worker.

Astonished visitors who experience this contact turn about quickly, looking for anyone close by who might have tried to get their attention. Some people have been shaken when they see that no one else stands within the circular space.

Apparitions of people who once worked at the Hovden fish cannery appear at these boilers inside the Monterey Bay Aquarium.

THE GHOST LADY OF THE LIGHT

Point Pinos Lighthouse
Asilomar Avenue near Del Monte Boulevard
Pacific Grove 93950
831-648-3176
http://www.ci.pg.ca.us/lighthouse/default.htm

Lighthouses always have a ghost story attached to them. Like old ships and theaters, spirits find them hard to leave even when hardship, disappointment, and loneliness were frequent and long-lasting features of the lives lived in these places. In the case of lighthouses, lighthouse keepers experienced long periods of isolation with occasional dangers arising from the rocky and stormy coasts they guarded.

An exception may be found at Point Pinos Lighthouse, where a female lighthouse keeper, Emily Fish, entertained visitors with piano recitals and served exotic tea to guests as they marveled at the spectacular view of the ocean. Known as the "socialite light keeper," Emily's day-to-day tranquil existence at beautiful Point Pinos, broken regularly by her parties and carriage rides, may have been enough to entice her spirit to remain on duty long after her death.

Opened on February 1, 1855, Point Pinos Lighthouse is the oldest continuously operating light station on the West Coast. Its first keeper was Charles Layton. Housing Layton, his wife, and four children, the tiny residence must have been crowded and, at times, noisy. Layton's tenure was, unfortunately, short lived. In November of 1856, while riding with the sheriff's posse in pursuit of bandit Anastacio Garcia, he was killed in a shootout. His widow, Charlotte, assumed her husband's duties until 1860 when she married her assistant, George Harris. Some ghost hunters speculate that Charlotte's ghost creates the bizarre sounds and fragrances that have been detected on the second floor of the residence and in the kitchen.

Emily Fish became keeper in 1893 after her husband died. She held the post until 1914 when poor health made it impossible for her to maintain the facility. Although Emily died elsewhere, docents and visitors believe her ghost wanders about second-floor rooms, moving objects, leaving the fragrance of her perfume, and creating the swishing sound of her long skirts.

Point Pinos Lighthouse in Pacific Grove may be haunted by ghosts of former lighthouse keepers.

I have not found anyone who has seen an apparition in the Point Pinos Lighthouse, but there are many people around Pacific Grove who will swear the place is haunted. Over the course of more than 20 visits, I've always found a docent or visitors who voluntarily raise the possibility of ghostly activity. During my trips, I've often encountered a female presence on the second floor and in the parlor. At times, the swish of her skirt can be easily heard as she moves across the room.

THE LADY IN LACE

The Ghost Tree
17 Mile Drive near Pescadero Point, past Cypress Drive
Pebble Beach 93935

The ghostly image of a lady dressed in "flowing robes of lacy white" has been reported near a weathered, sun-bleached Monterey cypress tree in Pebble Beach. Witnesses have spotted her walking the centerline of the road and wandering near the cliff. To some, her gown resembles a wedding dress, with a short train dragging on the ground. Others report she wears a lacy white dressing robe that was popular with wealthy ladies in the 1920s.

The sudden appearance of this ghostly lady has caused several minor accidents as drivers skid to a stop or run off the road trying to avoid hitting her. After coming to stop, drivers and their passengers are unable to find any pedestrians in the area. One couple spotted the ghostly lady walk from a spot close to the ghost tree to the nearby cliff. She appeared not to notice them. As she walked with her head bowed, the witnesses concluded she was either drunk or in a trance. After she disappeared behind some rocks, they searched for her but found no trace.

Local ghost hunters believe the lady in the lacy white gown is the ghost of Dona Maria del Carmen Barreto, former owner of 4,000 acres in what is now the fabled community of Pebble Beach. It is said that Dona Maria grew tired of living in the remote area, so in 1842 she sold the land for $0.12 per acre. With her $500 profit, she built a house in town, at 615 Abrego Street, and became a popular member of Monterey society. Later in life, she regretted the sale of such valuable real estate for so little money. (Today, $500 would buy only one square yard of Pebble Beach land.) Feeling the land was still rightfully hers, the ghost of Dona Maria roams the place she loved best, a spot now marked with a grotesquely twisted, wind-sculpted tree. On foggy nights or under a full moon, the tree has a bizarre appearance, which creates a surreal atmosphere. At times like these, the ghost of the lady in lace, Dona Maria, walks her former estate. She does not notice passersby even when they speak to her. She seems to be savoring the land she loved, finding her way to it by some attachment to the ghost tree.

GHOST OF THE ROMANTIC ARTIST

La Playa Hotel
900 Camino Real at Eighth Street
Carmel 93921
831-624-6476
www.laplayahotel.com

Known by locals as the Grande Dame of Old Carmel, La Playa Hotel has a romantic past, which may explain some of the paranormal phenomena experienced by visitors and staff. Reports of ghostly activity posted on the Internet are sparse, incomplete, and often in error. They also fail to include the remarkable history of the original occupants of the building, which contribute a great deal to suspicions that the place is haunted.

The core structure of the current hotel was designed by its original owner in 1905, Christopher Jorgensen, and constructed by Ben Turner. Intended as a home for his wife, Angela Ghirardelli, and their two children, Virgil and Aime, the place has since been renovated and greatly expanded into a four-star inn with a spectacular location near Carmel Bay Beach. To those familiar with the building's history, it is easy to find remnants of the Jorgenson home and traces of the bohemian period in Carmel history. The ghosts that haunt this place are the spirits of Angela and her niece, Alida. There are several other spirits there; holdovers from the 1930s when the place was the most fashionable inn on fabled Monterey Peninsula.

Angela was a genuine heiress, in line to inherit a fortune from the San Francisco chocolate empire founded by her grandfather in the dusty Gold Rush town of Hornitos. When Christopher Jorgensen met her in 1881, he was an accomplished painter of landscapes and instructor at the California School of Fine Arts in San Francisco. For two years, their relationship was limited by the boundaries of student-teacher decorum. Throughout this time, she was drawn to Christopher by her fascination with his most renowned painting, *Along the Wharves*. After a respectable passage of time from graduation, Christopher courted the heiress, won approval of her powerful family, and married her in 1888. As husband and wife, and independently wealthy, they spent a few years in Italy studying art and then set up a studio in Yosemite. In 1905, the couple discovered the rugged beauty of Carmel and the fledging art community developing there around the artistic talents of poet George Sterling and photographer Arnold Genthe. Soon after the Jorgensens built their great house, the new bohemian community flourished with the addition of other talented residents, such as poet Robinson Jeffers, and luminaries, including Jack London, Upton Sinclair, Charles Stoddard, Joaquin Miller, Mary Austin, Sinclair

Lewis, Sydney Yard, Mary Morgan, and the Jorgenson's niece, promising artist Alida Ghirardelli.

By all accounts, the Jorgenson home was a happy and busy place until August 8, 1909, when Alida went for her daily swim in Carmel Bay. That day, the undertow and tide were stronger than usual, causing Alida to struggle against the water until she drowned. Devastated by the death of their beloved niece, the Jorgensens left their Carmel home and returned to the San Francisco Bay Area. Christopher died on June 25, 1935. The following year, on February 11, 1936, Angela died in the same room, gazing at Christopher's painting *Along the Wharves*, which first attracted her to the love of her life.

Upon her death, Angela Ghirardelli Jorgensen returned to her beloved Carmel home. The pale apparition of a woman in ankle-length skirts has been seen by several visitors and employees in the lobby near the great fireplace. The woman moves slowly about the lobby, always facing the painting above the fireplace. The same apparition has been spotted outside, on the garden terrace, moving about as if she is greeting guests who have arrived at her home.

The other female apparition roaming the former Jorgensen mansion is that of Alida Ghirardelli. In spite of her position as one the of the heirs of the chocolate fortune founded by her grandfather, Alida was a true bohemian, walking about barefoot, swimming alone in the ocean, pursuing her art without regard for critics or rivals, and unmarried at the age of 29 when she died. Alida appears in the doorway separating the lobby from the restaurant and on the terrace. Her long hair appears wet and tangled as if she has just returned from her daily swim in Carmel Bay.

Several other ghosts have been spotted on the terrace. Many years ago, while relaxing on the terrace in a chaise, with the soft Carmel sun on my face, I slipped into a trance. Opening my eyes, I became aware of at least 20 people milling about as though they were at a party. The women wore long skirts while the men were dressed in high collars and tight coats typical of Edwardian styles. I believe I glimpsed a moment from the 1920s when Carmel was becoming a bastion for the wealthy from San Francisco and Los Angeles.

GHOST OF THE OLD BOHEMIANS

Pine Inn
Ocean Avenue at Monte Verde Street
Carmel 93921
831-624-3851
www.pineinn.com

In 1889, Pine Inn opened as a rustic inn on Junnipero Street constructed of wood from the old Tivoli Opera House in San Francisco. Thirteen years later, the entire building was rolled down the hill on logs to a new location closer to the ocean. This bold and hazardous project was successful, and the upgraded inn became an important center for the art colony that formed the nucleus of Carmel society. After several rounds of major renovations, starting in 1920 and continuing through the early 1990s, the structure doesn't resemble early photographs of the original inn. Today, Pine Inn is a high-end hotel with spectacular décor and a world-class restaurant. The oldest portions of the inn, however, retain the peculiar atmosphere of Carmel's early bohemian days, complete with spirits of some of the famous writers, painters, sculptors, actors, and poets of the town's art colony.

The founders of Carmel's bohemian society were noted poet George Sterling and photographer Arnold Genthe. These magnetic personalities attracted friends, colleagues, and associates from San Francisco and Los Angeles to the rugged beauty and intellectually liberated environment of the Monterey Peninsula, creating a critical mass that has sustained local artists through both world wars and the Depression. Among the luminaries who spent a great deal of time at Pine Inn in the early 20th century are Sinclair Lewis, Joaquin Miller, Mary Austin, Upton Sinclair, and Jack London.

Of all of these personalities, George Sterling and Jack London were, perhaps, the most tragic of the art colony. Best friends, they spent many months together wandering the rugged coastline of Carmel probing the depths of the literary arts, exploring nature, and soaking up the wisdom of fellow writers. By 1900, London had achieved worldwide fame while Sterling, highly acclaimed by critics, was little known outside of California. In spite of their successes, these famous writers were always one step ahead of their personal demons, and both are believed to have committed suicide. London's death on November 22, 1916, at his ranch in Glen Ellen sent Sterling into a downward spiral of depression. Always struggling against his illness, he continued to produce poetry until his suicide. He died of cyanide poisoning in his room, at the Bohemian Club in San Francisco, on the anniversary of London's death in 1926.

In death, George Sterling returned to his beloved Carmel and his room at Pine Inn. On the second floor of the inn, his ghost generates intense feelings of sadness and despair. Sensitives easily detect a thickened atmosphere, which, if entered, immediately creates depression and a forlorn sense of loss. This cloud of misery moves throughout the upper floors of the inn.

On the first floor, the apparition of a woman has been spotted sitting close to the fireplace near the lobby. This ghost generates sensations of comfort and happiness as if she is pleased to remain where she experienced the greatest joys of her life. If she is the ghost of novelist, playwright, and feminist Mary Austin (1868-1934), ghost hunters should look for her long dark hair flowing from beneath a hat, described as a Smokey-the-Bear hat, that she received from her friend Jack London.

GHOSTS OF THE FOUNDING FATHER

Mission San Carlos Borromeo de Carmelo
River Road at Lasuen Drive
Carmel 93921
831-624-1271

The first time I saw the Mission San Carlos Borromeo de Carmelo I felt weak in the knees. I was overwhelmed by its size, beauty, age, and history contained within its walls. Dazed and shaken by the realization that this structure has stood since the American Revolution, I wondered, if the Spanish mission could talk, what a fantastic view of history it could reveal. Today, the place still captures my imagination, offering a few ghosts that reveal glimpses of past centuries.

Founded in Monterey on June 3, 1770, by Father Juniper Serra, the mission began as a crude hut of mud and tree limbs under the flag of the King of Spain. In December of 1771, Father Serra relocated the mission close to the Carmel River to separate the soldiers of the presidio from the Indians who had come under the care of the priests. An adobe chapel was constructed with several buildings for dormitories, a library, and kitchen. In 1789, the church was destroyed by fire. This opened the way for construction of the massive church standing today. Completed in 1794 and constructed of sandstone by master stonemason Manuel Ruiz, with the help of Indian labor, the Mission Carmel community flourished until Mexico gained its independence from Spain on April 9, 1822. Under Mexican rule, the power of the church declined and the economic center of the region relocated to Monterey.

By 1842, the mission buildings were no longer occupied, and a long, slow period of decay set in. The cemetery, filled with the graves of hundreds of Indians and several priests and monks, was covered in weeds and mud. Doors, shutters, tiles, and other reusable building materials were removed and incorporated into new buildings in both Monterey and the Carmel River Valley. By the late 19th century, the mission lay in ruins and spawned many ghost stories that circulated around Monterey.

Local writer and historian Randall Reinstedt has written stories about teenaged boys who spent a night in the ruins on a dare. Frightened by shadows, the sound of the wind in the ruins of the bell tower, and small animals creeping around the place, the boys lost track of one another only to discover one of their friends dead. It is said the ghost of the boy walked the mission ruins for decades and sometimes shows up for 21st-century visitors as a fog approximating the shape of a man.

For more than 100 years, visitors, church employees, and museum docents have witnessed strange sights, which lead to only one conclusion—the place is haunted.

The small size of the cemetery on the north-west side of the church belies the fact that hundreds of Indians are buried there. Their unmarked graves hold the remains of a people who were subjugated by the priests, often treated as slaves, only to die of disease brought to their pristine land by Europeans. These unknown people are joined by several priests, church officials, and employees who rest in marked graves. As expected, sensitive visitors feel the weight of the ages when they enter the cemetery and the touch of a few ghosts, too. A common experience is a touch on the arm or shoulder by invisible hands. Often, this encounter is preceded by musty odors of rotting leather, hemp, and sage.

A local historian who joined the spirit world years ago made one of the most important sightings of a ghost at Mission Carmel. Randall Reinstedt recorded the man's encounter. While sitting on a bench in the front courtyard, the historian spotted a man dressed as a priest walking toward the church. Sensing something familiar about the man, the historian approached him only to see the robed figure disappear into a wall.

The image of another priest, one dressed in 18th-century robe or Cossack and resembling Father Serra, has been spotted in several locations around the mission and inside the church during New Year's Eve services. The ghost has been spotted walking through the door of the stone building to the right of the church, then disappearing. I've seen that apparition three times—once inside the church, once in the

Built in 1771, Mission San Carlos de Boromeo in Carmel may be haunted by its founder, Father Junipero Serra.

courtyard near the cemetery, and a third time inside the reconstructed dormitory where Father Serra once lived. Each time, the image was full-bodied, dressed in brown robes and sandals, and translucent without being transparent. The ghost did not appear to notice me as I spoke to him, but when I moved to within five feet of him, he vanished, leaving only a cold spot.

The ghost of a priest who served the church in the first decade of the 20th century walks the mission grounds, too. During repair of the church roof, a small building currently used as a museum was used as a chapel. For many months, candles burned only slightly in Friday evening services were found Saturday morning completely melted. An investigation by two men who worked at the mission revealed that the candles were lit at a time when all doors were locked and sealed. These men witnessed the glow of candlelight through the windows at a time when they were certain no living being had entered the building. The experience left them with the conclusion that a long-dead priest was returning to the temporary chapel each week to light candles and say prayers for parishioners he left behind.

GHOST OF THE WHITE LADY

Monastery Beach
1.5 miles south of the intersection of Highway 1 and Rio Road
Carmel 93921

Just over the hill from central Carmel, Highway 1 runs south through artichoke fields and past one of the most popular and dangerous locales for scuba diving in California. Monastery Beach is known for its steep slope to the water's edge, pounding surf, and lush marine life, which includes otters, reef-dwelling creatures of all kinds, and sharks. I taught scuba classes there for many years, taking experienced divers into the most challenging of conditions and revealing to them one of the best dive spots on the coast.

Named for the Carmelite Monastery nestled amid tall trees on the east side of the highway, Monastery Beach has been the scene of several diving-related fatalities. Many of us who participated in body recovery operations wondered if the ghosts of dead divers would haunt this beautiful beach. The ghost that inhabits the site, however, is believed to be a nun or novitiate from the monastery, or a hitchhiker who happened to be wearing a hooded sweatshirt or cape when she died on or near the highway.

I recall numerous times when I watched traffic on busy Highway 1 come to a halt as a group of women, clad in the black and white garments typical of nuns, crossed the road for a respite on the beach. Locals with whom I was familiar mentioned that, in the 1960s, one or two of the women had been hit by cars driven by people distracted by the pounding surf or other traffic.

Motorists passing by Monastery Beach at night have taken evasive action to avoid hitting what they describe as a ghostly figure walking across the street. The figure always walks toward the beach, appears in the southbound lane, and wears a scarf or hood over her head. When panicked drivers screech to a halt and look back at the roadway to find no one there.

Other places to hunt ghosts:

CAPTAIN'S INN

8122 Moss Landing Road
Moss Landing 95039
831-633-5550
www.captainsinn.com

Located in the quiet village of Moss Landing, this modest mansion was built in 1906 and initially used as offices for the Pacific Coast Steamship Company. With overnight accommodations established on the second floor for visiting sailing masters and captains, the current name of the bed and breakfast inn is historically appropriate. The manger of the place told me she has had no paranormal experiences in the building, but she admits that odd things happen. When I visited the inn, I encountered a female presence in a guest room on the north side of the second floor, at the front of the building.

JOHN DENVER CRASH SITE

On the beach at Ocean View Avenue between Acropolis Street and
  Asilomar Avenue
Pacific Grove 93950

October 12, 1997, was a sad day for me. My friend John Denver
took off from Monterey Peninsula Airport in an experimental
airplane; climbed out over the blue Pacific Ocean, parallel to the
Pacific Grove coast; then crashed into the sea. His plane hit the water
about 150 yards offshore. A few witnesses on the beach described the
rapid descent and impact. Their vantage point is now the site of an
informal shrine composed of flowers, charms, pictures, John's albums,
and other offerings. I don't believe that John's ghost visits this place,
but the highly charged emotions of his admirers have left interesting
remnants or imprints there. I've seen some bizarre light anomalies that
were reportedly captured in digital images when sensitives detected
intense sadness. This fascinating phenomenon is paranormal and
commonly found in cemeteries, but it has nothing to do with ghosts.

MONTEREY COMMERCIAL PIER

Fisherman's Wharf
Del Monte Avenue
Monterey 93940

Several visitors to this busy commercial wharf have reported
seeing ghosts of old fishermen. Typically, these ghosts appear sitting
on benches gazing out to sea as if they are pondering the return of
a ship or their body. Some of these apparitions have spoken when
spoken to. No specific identification of any of these ghosts has been
made. During the century this wharf has been in use, countless
fishermen and boatmen have departed the safety of their moorings
only to lose their lives at sea. There have been fatal accidents on the
pier as well.

The best time to see apparitions on Fisherman's Wharf is late at
night when boating operations have closed and few people are around.
Discovery of some of these apparitions may be preceded by noxious

odors such as rotting seaweed or fish. Such odors do occur naturally on commercial fishing piers, but when the sweet scent of salt air suddenly changes without a breeze or other cause, look for a ghost.

CEMETERIO EL ENCINAL

Fremont Street at Camino Aquijito
Monterey 93940
831-646-3864

Contrary to popular belief, cemeteries aren't good places to find ghosts. Spirits of the dead show up only if their monument or grave is damage by natural phenomena, desecrated by thieves, or defaced by vandals. The paranormal occurrence detected by sensitives is usually the result of environmental imprints of intense, repetitive emotions experienced by grieving friends and family members. Strong imprints can be perceived at the final resting place of Edward "Doc" Ricketts (1897-1948) in the columbarium, the grave of Cannery Row madam Flora Woods-Adams (1876-1948), and at the grave of theater builder Jack Swan (1817-1896). These imprints may be cold spots, isolated cells of intense sadness, or EVP of sobbing.

GHOSTS OF THE CHINESE WHALERS

Whaling Station
Point Lobos State National Reserve
Carmel 93923
831-624-4909

A thriving whaling industry once occupied Whaler's Cove on land that now comprises the world-famous Point Lobos State National Reserve. From 1852 to 1879, ships anchored in the cove and discharged cargoes of bloody whale carcasses and barrels of whale oil. On the rocky beaches, giant "try pots" rendered blunder into the oil that fueled the lamps of Carmel and Monterey. The whaler's cabin remains as a remnant of the industry. Filled with artifacts, including whale bones, from the 1800s, the place is also filled with ghosts.

GHOST OF THE QUICKSAND MAN

Underwood-Brown Adobe
Pacific Avenue at Madison Street
Monterey 93940

Built in 1843 by prominent citizen Santiago Stokes and occupied by Jose Maria Sanchez, this house looks mundane, but it is the site of some very spooky paranormal activity. Jose Sanchez lived in the house until 1852 when he suffered an "accidental" death. After massing a fortune in gold believed to be as large as $85,000, Sanchez was cursed by a local witch who had taken the side of the man's adversaries. Ignoring the curse, Jose walked out the house one day and disappeared into a previously unnoticed pit of quicksand. His stash of gold, which remains undiscovered, has added to the mystique of this house. Many visitors have experienced the ghost of Sanchez, which is said to wander the place guarding his hidden wealth.

GHOSTS OF THE OLD SIMPSON'S RESTAURANT

Fifth Avenue at San Carlos Street
Carmel 93921
831-624-5755

Constructed in the 1920s and used as a boarding house, the building has been the home of Simpson's Restaurant since 1959. Among the ghosts who reportedly show up here is the building's first owner, a lady dressed in an ankle-length skirt and blouse with puffy sleeves. Ghostly images of a cook have been spotted in the kitchen. Local writer Randall Reinstedt has reported that tables 9 and 10 have been the scene of paranormal activity, including disappearing silverware and relish trays and glasses turned upside down.

CHAPTER 4

The Central Coast:
Big Sur, San Simeon, Cayucos, and Morro Bay

Big Sur gets its name from the Spanish who sailed its coast for two centuries before attempting to colonize the area. Its sheer cliffs that meet the sea in swirling foam, uninterrupted by safe anchorages, kept the region in the hands of local Indians until Portola's ships landed in Monterey in 1770. Still isolated at the dawn of the 19th century, the Spanish called the unwelcoming coast *el pais del sur,* "the big country to the south" of Monterey. In common usage, the term became *el sur grande,* or "the big south." Rumored to be rich in natural resources, the land was also considered impenetrable and designated on maps as unexplored. Today, we call it Big Sur. Although the name designates a small community 30 miles south of Carmel, the entire coast as far south as Cambria has been referred to as the Big Sur Coast.

This once forbidding stretch of coast is now traversed by California's Highway 1, also known as the Pacific Coast Highway. Conveying awe-struck visitors in cars, RVs, and on bicycles, a trip north or south on Highway 1 offers spectacular scenery, a chance to explore uninhabited beaches, fascinating pioneer structures, and a few world-famous restaurants. The combination of big sky, the endless expanse of the Pacific Ocean, rugged mountains, and several haunted locations make the Big Sur Coast irresistible to people traveling between southern and northern California who have a little time on their hands and a curiosity about remote haunted places. I've traveled this coast, between Morro Bay and Carmel, many times by car, bicycle, and boat and always discovered something new and fascinating, and often paranormal.

PHANTOM BELLS OF THE LEAD HORSE

Garrapata State Park
Highway 1, 8 miles south of Carmel Highlands
Mal Paso Creek Road

The name of this road is a clue that something awful happened here in the past. *Mal paso* is Spanish for "bad crossing." Today, the words are joined together, but the Mal Paso Creek Road and nearby trails still give local hikers chills as they recall stories of disasters and hear phantom bells.

Sitting between Carmel and tranquil Big Sur, the rugged mountain region was once owned by two soldiers who retired in the 1830s. They were awarded the property via a Mexican land grant. Over the next 40 years, only a few settlers entered the area, purchasing bits of land and carving out a living in the arid highlands. In the 1880s, coal mines were opened at the head of Mal Paso Creek and tanbark was harvested from nearby groves of oak trees. Soon, a steady stream of heavily laden wagons traveled the treacherous Palo Colorado Canyon Road to Notley's Landing near Point Lobos to discharge their cargo.

In 1898, one unlucky driver lost control of his four-horse rig while traveling the narrow, winding road. Some stories say the cargo was coal while the majority of them specify several tons of tanbark. In either case, the steep road, slippery from dense morning fog, and worn brakes caused the wagon to gain speed, nearly dragging the panicked horses around a sharp turn. Failing to make the turn, the entire rig, including the driver, flew off the road into the creek below. Neither the driver nor the horses survived.

A short time after this disaster, other drivers moving along the creek-side road reported hearing the sound of bells. When the stories of the strange bells spread, fears and superstitions ran rampant, as it was recalled that the dead driver had tied bells to the collar of his lead horse.

As recently as 2007, hikers who traversed the trails that cross Mal Paso Creek reported hearing the bells of the lead horse that died in 1898. Local historian and writer Randall Reinstedt reported sightings of astonished hikers dashing out of the way of a run-away horse-drawn wagon as it barreled down Palo Colorado Canyon Road.

GHOST OF THE TB GIRL

Point Sur Lighthouse
Highway 1
Big Sur 93920
831-625-4419
www.bigsurcalifornia.org/pointsur.html

Sitting atop a volcanic knoll connected to the mainland by a sandy spit, Point Sur Lighthouse is listed among the top 10 haunted lighthouses in America. Aside from its reputation for ghostly activity, its fascinating history, spectacular location, and unsurpassed views of the coast make this locale an essential stop for ghost hunters who travel Highway 1 between Carmel and Morro Bay.

Built in 1889 in response to the disastrous sinking of the steamships SS *Los Angeles* in 1873 and the *Ventura* in 1875, the light remains in service today as an automated vital aid to navigation. Even with the lighthouse fully operational, 15 disastrous shipwrecks have occurred near Point Sur, the last on May 14, 1956. The last lighthouse keeper left in 1974. The California State Parks system maintains the light tower and keeper's three-story house and conducts tours, including moonlight tours on selected dates. An evening ghost visit is offered each year during the last days of October with storyteller Kevin Hanstick (see Appendix F).

Typically, lighthouses are haunted by the people who lived or

The lighthouse at Big Sur is haunted by a young girl and an old man who used to live in the keeper's quarters.

worked there. Such is the case with Point Sur Lighthouse, but there may be several spirits inside the tower, in the keeper's house, or on the grounds who lost their lives in one of the many disasters that occurred nearby. Airship crashes in 1915 (USS *H-3*) and 1935 (USS *Macon*) and several shipwrecks have generated plenty of spirits who might become attached to this beacon of salvation. One of the strangest disasters to occur near the lighthouse involved the coastal freight *Babinda*, on March 3, 1923. While sailing off the coast of Santa Cruz, the ship caught fire. Efforts to extinguish the blaze were ineffectual, so the crew abandoned the ship. As the fire raged, the ship continued sailing 40 miles south until it approached Point Sur Lighthouse. Only then, did the disintegrating ship founder and sink. This bizarre event has prompted many people to conclude that a ghost crew took over the ship and steered her to the graveyard of ships around Point Sur.

The most active ghost in the keeper's house is that of a teenaged girl who died of tuberculosis in a third-floor bedroom about 1900. After her death, her family moved away. Soon after the next keeper and his family moved in, a young boy complained that he could not sleep at night because of the loud coughing coming from the adjacent room. Night after night, the frustrated mother opened the room to show her troubled son that it was empty. Still, the coughing continued for years.

Another ghost on the property is that of a former keeper. This fellow shows up in the barn, at the water tower, and inside the keeper's house wearing his uniform and a white hat. He moves about without sound but creates intense cold spots in addition to an apparition that reveals the details of his clothing.

THE RUSH OF ANGELS' WINGS

Nepenthe
48510 Highway 1
Big Sur 93920
831-667-2345
www.nepenthebigsur.com

In Homer's *Odyssey, nepenthes* is mentioned as a magical potion, a drug, given to Helen of Troy by the Queen of Egypt. Apart from the fictional elements of Homer's great work, the potion he mentions has a basis in fact. Ancient Egyptian analgesics, or painkillers, were described in Greek medical books under the term *nepenthes pharmakon.*

The word *nepenthe* was aptly chosen as a name for Lolly and Bill Fassett's incredible restaurant perched on the steep slopes of the Santa Lucia Mountains and literally hanging over the beautiful Pacific Ocean. People who visit the restaurant feel liberated from worldly concerns, as if some magical potion has transported them to a mystical land of incomprehensible beauty. I don't have any evidence that Nepenthe is haunted, but there is something spiritual going on there that may interest paranormal enthusiasts.

During one of my visits to Nepenthe, I ran into my old friend John Denver. Typically in a hurry and distracted by countless obligations, John was unusually slow-paced that day, and we spent more than an hour eating lunch.

Around the middle of the afternoon, while sitting on the terrace and enjoying the sun on our faces, he asked, "Do you feel that?"

"Feel what?" I responded with a whisper, not wanting to break the peace of the moment.

This spectacular sculpture depicting the phoenix in flight, stands at Nepenthe and, to many visitors, symbolizes the magical nature of the place.

"It's the rush of wings. Angels' wings. When you hear that, something fantastic will happen."

Moments of silence passed as I listened. There was no wind that afternoon, only a soft hum drifted through the air. Clearing my head with a brief meditation, I heard the flutter of feathers and felt the air move across my face.

"Now," John said quietly. "There is something here, now."

Rising from our chairs on the terrace, we walked to the edge and looked down nearly 500 feet to the ocean below. The image of what we saw still gives me chills. Swimming from north to south, barely 50 yards offshore was a herd of dolphin. As other amazed guests crowded around us, we watched for more than 30 minutes as the herd passed, churning the blue Pacific into dazzling white foam. One man in the crowd, a biologist, estimated that more than 3,000 dolphins swam by Nepenthe that afternoon. Almost overcome by the magic of what we saw, John and I were speechless when the end of the herd passed us. Trailing the last dolphin were three massive gray whales, blowing water high into the air.

Later in the day, after John had departed, I wondered how the rush of angels' wings was connected to the fantastic appearance of the dolphins and whales. I could not think of a reason why the two were connected, but the process of thinking about it left me in a daze—as if I were numbed by potion. It was the spell of Nepenthe, a place so beautiful and magical that angels or some other benevolent paranormal beings, stir the air over the terrace to foretell the approach of something fantastic.

GHOSTS OF THE WHITE FIGURES

Piedras Blancas Lighthouse
15950 Cabrillo Highway (Highway 1)
San Simeon 93452

Standing on a rocky promontory north of San Simeon, Piedras Blancas Lighthouse was erected in 1875 to guide ships around the treacherous waters of Point Conception. Standing 142 feet above sea, its light signature of one flash every 15 seconds can be seen 25 miles from shore. A two-story Victorian house was built nearby to house the keeper and his family. Norman Francis was the last civilian lighthouse keeper before the United States Coast Guard assumed control of the lighthouse in 1939. The light was automated in 1978, and the grounds were leased to the U.S. Fish and Wildlife Service. Today, the site is owned by the Bureau of Land Management and supported by Friends of Piedras Blancas Lighthouse. The building is open for tours.

None of the people I spoke to at the lighthouse would confirm reports of white, transparent figures standing near the edge of the cliffs gazing out to sea. These figures reveal few details, appearing as though they are wearing a hooded robe or shroud. There is speculation the ghosts are victims of shipwrecks or nearby maritime disasters. A research of historical records revealed only three major nautical events near the lighthouse. On August 29, 1869, the *Harlech Castle* struck a submerged rock only 1.5 miles from the lighthouse. Several crewmen died while whalers from San Simeon rescued survivors. On October 17, 1869, the steamer *Sierra Nevada* sank three miles north of Piedras Blancas. In a historic naval engagement close to Piedras Blancas, on September 22, 1941, the tanker *Montebello* was torpedoed and sunk by a Japanese submarine. Only a few people lost their lives in these sea disasters, but they may stand with other spirits, unknown sailors lost overboard from small craft, at desolate Piedras Blancas.

HEARST CASTLE

750 Hearst Castle Road (at Highway 1)
San Simeon 93452-9740
1-800-444-4445
www.hearstcastle.com/tours/

Hearst Castle is one of the greatest American architectural achievements. Conceived by media mogul William Randolph Hearst in 1919 and built between 1919 and 1947 by architect Julia Morgan, the place is a massive monument to opulence and excess. Comprised of 56 bedrooms, 61 bathrooms, 19 sitting rooms, several dining rooms, dens, a large movie theater, and kitchens, the 60,000-square-foot mansion contains priceless art, antiques, ornate ceilings, wall panels, doors, and fireplaces from European castles. Indoor pools and the famous outdoor Neptune pool, decorated with the facade of an authentic Roman temple, allow guests to exercise and cool off while they admire the spectacular views of the ocean and surrounding Santa Lucia Mountains. Three large guesthouses carried on the themes of the main house with antique ceilings, antiques, and bathrooms with authentic Roman tiles. Although the home was formally named La Cuesta Encantada (the Enchanted Hill), Hearst and his companion, movie star Marion Davies, referred to the 250,000-acre estate as "the ranch," thinking of it as their vacation home in the country, away from the demands of running a media empire that included a Hollywood movie studio. Guests looked upon an invitation to Hearst Castle as a sure sign that they had achieved the highest social status attainable. The place was so elegant, and guests were so pampered, that playwright George Bernard Shaw said, "This is the way God would have done it if He had the money."

From the late 1920s through the early 1940s, a steady stream of famous guests arrived by plane or train for visits that sometimes lasted six weeks. Among the luminaries who enjoyed Hearst's world-class hospitality were the presidents Herbert Hoover, Calvin Coolidge, and Franklin Roosevelt; Winston Churchill; Orson Welles; Charles Lindberg; the Marx Brothers; Jimmy Stewart; Charlie Chaplin; Clark Gable; Bob Hope; and Cary Grant. With such notables coming and going, sometimes including gossip columnists such as Louella Parsons and famous reporters and a large house staff, it would seem unlikely that criminal activity might have occurred here that would lead to a haunting. At least one unsolved murder is linked to the castle and a second may have occurred on board Hearst's yacht, the *Oneida*. Added to these mysteries, some of the thousands of antiques and architectural remnants from ancient European castles, manor houses, and temples may have come with a ghost attached.

When questioned about paranormal activity inside the great castle or its guesthouses, staff members told me they had no information. An inquiry directed to the current owner, California's state park system, produced no response. Many people who have toured the

The world-famous Hearst Castle in San Simeon may be haunted by ghosts of movie stars and a murder victim.

The apparition of a woman has been spotted reclining in this bed at Hearst Castle.

place, however, have posted reports on the Internet and in newspaper articles. I've had several brushes with the paranormal in the great mansion. Ghost hunters may visit the castle only by guided tour. This severely restricts any paranormal investigation, but it is possible to lag behind the group of 20 to 40 visitors and snap photographs or try to capture EAP. Several fortunate visitors have spotted apparitions.

In William Hearst's master bedroom, the apparition of an elderly woman has been seen. Dressed in an elegant nightgown, she appears in the bed, reclining on a huge stack of pillows. This ghost has made eye contact with visitors and even gestures some to move closer to her bed. I spotted an apparition of this description standing in front of a mirror in one of the bedrooms, but I am uncertain which one. Apparitions of butlers and maids have been spotted in the kitchen, the grand dining room, and the gothic study.

Audio disturbances are easier to detect in the great mansion and in each of the guesthouses. Audio remnants of parties and other social events manifest as sound bursts of several people talking at once or musical notes from one of the many bands that entertained Hearst's guests. Cold spots can be found all over the place. These are not spirit manifestations but most likely places where intense emotions left environmental imprints.

It is not possible to openly conduct paranormal investigations of the estate, but based on historical accounts, it is likely that the ghost of a murder victim roams the grounds. In 1924, Abigail Kinsolving worked for Marion Davies as a private secretary. Being a trusted and much-liked young woman, she was often included in social events. One evening while cruising the southern California coast on the Hearst yacht, the 280-foot *Oneida,* Kinsolving claimed movie producer Thomas Ince raped her. That same night, Ince was taken ashore, with a doctor in attendance, supposedly because of a sudden, severe stomach ailment. At least one witness reported that he was bleeding when he left the *Oneida,* and several others on board the yacht believed he had been shot.

After leaving the yacht, Ince's condition worsened, and he died the next day at his Hollywood home. In their investigation, the police cited Abigail as a possible suspect, fostering various theories about the event that point to her as the shooter. When Ince's cause of death was recorded as a heart attack, Abigail was absolved of any involvement in Ince's death.

Several months later, Abigail Kinsolving gave birth to a baby girl and then died mysteriously when her car crashed into a tree on the Hearst estate. Two of Hearst's bodyguards discovered her body. A suicide note was found on the seat next to her body, but people at the scene who were familiar with Abigail's handwriting doubted its authenticity. Speculation began immediately that associates of Ince murdered Abigail. As the scandal grew, it was revealed that Kinsolving's baby girl, Louise, was placed in an orphanage supported by Marion Davies.

Today, unexplained light anomalies and pale, partial apparitions occurring near the road adjacent to the covered riding path are attributed to Abigail Kinsolving. Before visiting Hearst Castle, ghost hunters should watch the movie *The Cat's Meow*. It depicts the intrigue that took place on board the *Oneida* the night Tom Ince died.

GHOST OF CAPTAIN CASS

Cass House
222 North Ocean Avenue
Cayucos 93430
805-995-3669
www.casshouseinn.com

Abandoned for more than 20 years, the Cass House underwent a spectacular 14-year renovation, beginning in 1995, and the ghost of Captain Cass still walks the house that bears his name. Built in 1867 with a small fortune made from a long career aboard transatlantic merchant ships and the California lumber business, the captain's house was once the social center of the booming community of Cayucos. Attracting wealthy families from San Simeon and Morro Bay, events at the Cass House included holiday gatherings, weddings, and musical recitals.

It is unclear when the last of the Cass family left Cayucos, but the house changed hands a few times in the early 20th century before it was abandoned in the 1970s. The once elaborate San Francisco "stick" style house became severely worn and weathered by the harsh maritime climate, taking on the appearance of a haunted house. Boarded-up windows, scraps of fallen shingles in the yard, complete dissolution of the once spectacular exterior paint, and a yard full of tall weeds gave locals and tourists alike the impression that the place was haunted. In fact, before renovation began, stories appeared in newspapers and magazines about ghost sightings at the Cass House.

Famed writer and ghost investigator Richard Senate visited the place with psychic Debbie Christenson who detected the captain's spirit. Through her psychic sensitivities, she determined that the captain was unhappy his grand house had become a slum. She also detected ghostly activity in the music room at the rear of the house.

The first report of ghostly activity in the house came only a few days after the captain's death in 1888. His niece made a written record of her experience when she entered the house with her husband one night. As the couple walked through the music room, a music box started to play, causing them to run from the house. During the many years the Cass House sat abandoned, several people reported that, as they peeked through the dirty windows at the rear of the house, they heard the sounds of a piano and a violin. Psychics have seen ghostly musical instruments in the vacant room.

When the place was opened in 2007 as the Cass House Restaurant and Inn, reports of ghostly activity increased. Patrons and staff get the impression that the former owner is present and pleased with the salvation and beautiful renovation of his home. Some astonished guests have reported witnessing the apparition of the captain, complete with his white beard, commander's hat, and chest sash. The common paranormal experience at the Cass House is the sound of instruments in the former music room.

MORRO BAY HIGH SCHOOL

235 Atascadero Road
Morro Bay 93442
805-771-1845

In every city I've visited in the course of investigating paranormal phenomena, I've run across reports of a haunted high school. These stories typically include the tragic suicide of a student or the sudden death of a custodian or teacher. It is easy to dismiss these stories when a search of local newspaper archives and interviews with teachers and staff fail to turn up any credible reports of a death on campus. Therefore, when I heard Morro Bay High School had a ghost, I suspected the stories were the product of youthful imaginations.

Various sources report that a boy died after falling to the floor while trying to climb a rope anchored to the rafters 20 feet overhead. Local newspaper archives are poorly filed and offer no information about such a tragedy. A colleague who lives in San Luis Obispo County investigated the story for me and came up with some interesting observations. Many people may have detected cold spots in the gym, but no collaborative findings, such as examinations by experts or accurate accounts by reliable witnesses, could be obtained. My colleague was able to spend time alone in the gym in the early evening, when the place was deserted and the lights turned off. She observed a ball of light floating over the floors, moving slowly from one end of the gym to the other. The phenomenon continued for about five minutes, and then the light faded into the darkness.

Is this high school gym haunted? The light anomaly is compelling and serves as basis for further investigation. Keep in mind that visitors to California public schools must check in at the office and receive permission to walk the grounds.

GHOST OF THE GEEZER

Legends at the Circle Inn Bar
899 Main Street
Morro Bay 93442
805-772-2525

This popular Morro Bay watering hole has been upgraded to sports bar status, but many locals remember when the Circle Inn was a run-down dive. Its clientele included fishermen, commercial divers, boat operators, and an assortment of bizarre characters who simply would not fit in at the other bars in town that catered to tourists. Many years ago, I spent a lot of time at the Circle Inn Bar. While gathering research material for a novel about fishermen and whales, I became a regular at the bar, talking with the locals and soaking up the rhythms and tones of their speech and unique aspects of their character while noting their drinking habits. One character stands out as most memorable because I had contact with him before and after his death.

Ronald was a retired deck hand who had spent most of his life at sea, working the weather decks of fishing boats from Oxnard to Monterey. At the age of 60, he looked 80, worn and weathered from hard work and too much alcohol. Ronald was a quiet man who drank slowly but spent many hours at it each day. Late one evening, I entered the Circle Inn Bar and exchanged quiet hellos and nods with Ronald. He then lifted his beer from the bar and staggered to one of the booths along the north wall that was almost obscured by the darkness of the place. A few minutes later, the din of hushed conversations at the bar was broken by the sound of a glass hitting the floor. Everyone seated at the bar turned around to find Ronald slumped forward on the table, with his glass shattered on the floor amid a pool of beer. Quiet chuckles flowed about the bar as if this had happened before. But something didn't look right. Even in the darkness, Ronald's weathered face looked pale. Paramedics were called, but when they arrived, it was clear that Ronald had died.

A few days later, I returned to the establishment and took my place at the bar, chatting with some fishermen from Oregon. While we talked, I heard the unmistakable sound of a glass hitting the floor. Turning around, I saw no one sitting in Ronald's death booth nor did I see anything on the floor. The next night, I heard the breaking glass again, but this time, I saw the partial apparition of Ronald sitting in the corner booth along the north wall. Amazed by the apparition, I left my barstool and walked slowly toward Ronald's booth. As I approached, he looked at me and said, "You know me?" and then he faded away.

I later heard that several Circle Inn Bar patrons and staff had seen Ronald's apparition and heard the breaking beer glass. With the transformation of the inn into a sports bar, Ronald's booth has been replaced by modern furniture. His transparent, partial apparition still appears near the north wall, as if he is still seated in that dark booth, nursing his beer.

GHOST LADY IN BLACK

Black Lake
Near Pacific Coast Highway at Callender Road
Oceano 93445

Isolation from distant city lights and rugged terrain make Black Lake one of the scariest places to visit at night. It is even scarier if you go there searching for the ghost of a woman who may have drowned in the lake during the Mexican period (1820-1846). Tall reeds near the shore, cold breezes from the nearby ocean, and strange sounds from unseen critters make you think something paranormal and evil lurks nearby. But if you can set aside such fears and visit the place with a few reliable colleagues who are not easily frightened, you may glimpse this fascinating ghost.

The unsubstantiated story tells of a wealthy Mexican woman whose children drowned in the lake. Grief-stricken, she ventured out on the water in an unstable canoe, searching for her children. Continuing her search after sunset, strong ocean breezes churned the surface of the lake into wavelets, causing the canoe to tip over. The grieving mother was dumped into the frigid water and drowned.

It has been reported that she shows up most nights, about 12:30 A.M., floating a few inches above the surface of Black Lake. Witnesses describe her clothing as a fancy, black Victorian dress with ruffled shoulders, a high collar, and a full skirt. Those who have gotten a good look at her say she wears long jeweled earrings and her hair is gathered in a tight bun on the back of her head. They also claim that she does not have a face. In its place is an oval of white light. This characteristic is commonplace in Hispanic ghost lore.

This ghost first appears near the center of the lake and then moves toward visitors on the shore. She never moves onto land, but vanishes while still hovering over the water. This ghost makes no sound, but her appearance frightens ducks and other waterfowl.

Renowned ghost hunter and writer Richard Senate has visited Black Lake with a psychic and others who claimed to have seen this ghost on more than one occasion. One of his witnesses reported that during a previous visit, she and three companions saw the ghost at the same time. Senate was unable to gather evidence of ghostly activity, but one of his colleagues experienced something so fearful that she broke into sobs and bolted for the safety of her car.

The lady of Black Lake may be the same ghost that shows up a short distance from the lake northwest of Callender Road. In this location, the female ghost appears dressed in a long white gown. There is speculation that this "white lady" is the ghost of a woman whose husband and children died in a tragic car crash on nearby Highway 1. I could not locate any newspaper accounts of an accident at this location within the past 20 years.

If you plan to hunt for the Lady in Black, first visit the location during daylight hours to become familiar with the terrain. Study maps and satellite images of the area, taking note of the other small lakes nearby. Take at least two reliable flashlights with you and a cell phone for emergencies. The lake is not far from Highway 1, but help is not readily available.

Other places to hunt for ghosts:

GHOST OF THE CORN MASK

Fernwood Campground
47200 Highway 1
Big Sur 93920
831-667-2422

Once the home of the Esalen Indians, this popular campground offers rustic campsites and tents to serious hikers and others who want to get close to nature in Big Sur. Trails take hikers through some spectacular country, including redwood groves, the Big Sur River, and a 60-foot waterfall. The ghost of an Indian shaman walks through the tent campground in the middle of the night. He wears a corn husk mask and clothing made of tanned skins and furs. Gliding silently several inches above the ground, he is not threatening, but his apparition has caused some campers to leave in the middle of the night.

HOWLING GHOSTS

The Dunes
Morro Bay 93442

The long desolate stretch of sand dunes that separate Morro Bay from the Pacific Ocean can be accessed only by boat. The adventure is well worth the effort for ghost hunters who want to experience the screaming spirits of the dunes. These distressed spirits may be victims of maritime disasters whose bodies washed ashore over the past two centuries. To visit the dunes, rent a kayak and life preserver and paddle across the estuary at high tide. At low tide, your kayak will run aground, and you will have to traverse a long stretch of sticky mud to get to dry sand. Be mindful of the tide or the return trip to the dock will be arduous and hazardous, especially for inexperienced kayakers.

CHAPTER 5

The South-Central Coast:
Gaviota, Los Olivos, Santa Maria, and San Luis Obispo

Soon after the arrival of Spanish explorers in 1770, missions were established at Santa Barbara, La Purisima near present-day Lompoc, and San Luis Obispo that transformed the region into a vast agricultural domain. Under the supervision of mission *padres* and Spanish soldiers, thousands of Indians labored to produce leather, tallow, grain, and other products that were sent by ship to ports in Mexico, South America, and American coastal states. Many Indians died at an early age under the harsh rule of mission overseers and received nothing more than an unmarked grave as a final resting place. The spirits of many of these forgotten souls still roam mission grounds and fields and walk the aisles of the adobe churches they helped to construct. Ghosts of *padres,* soldiers, Yankee explorers and settlers, and some of the banditos that terrorized the region also show themselves at places like Mattei's in Los Olivos, La Cruces near Gaviota Pass, and at Mission La Purisima Concepcion near Lompoc. Ghosts from more contemporary periods haunt the Burger King in Lompoc and the world-famous Andersen's Split Pea Soup Restaurant in Buellton.

GHOSTS OF THE MEXICAN GIRLS

Gaviota Beach
Gaviota Beach Road
Gaviota 93117
805-968-1033

If you do an online search for information about ghosts in the Gaviota area, you will run across a brief mention of the "ghost bridge." Spanning the Gaviota Creek watershed from one promontory to another, the bridge was built in the late 1890s. The fact that it has remained standing for more than a century through powerful earthquakes and several storms, floods, and fires has inspired local rangers to call it the "ghost bridge." I could not find any information about paranormal phenomena associated with it, however. There is no record of train wrecks or suicides to suggest the bridge may harbor a ghost or phantom. The Gaviota Creek campground, however, is haunted. I learned that by personal experience.

During my summer bicycle trips between Los Angeles and San Francisco, I spent several nights in a sleeping bag in the windy Gaviota Creek campground. One night, my companion and I were awakened by the distant sound of a child crying. Since it was the middle of the week and very late in the summer, we were certain we were the only people spending the night at the campground. With flashlights in hand, we searched the area but found nothing. It appeared that no one had entered the campground after we had turned in for the night.

Minutes after returning to our sleeping bags, the crying resumed, but it sounded much closer. Sitting up, I was astonished to see two children appear out of the darkness, walking toward me. Walking hand in hand, they appeared to be girls with long black hair draped over their shoulders. As they moved closer, I could see they were wearing long, white, shapeless dresses that may have been nightgowns. When I shined the beam of my flashlight upon them, the light passed right through them. A moment later, they vanished. Still astonished by the experience, I asked my cycling companion if he had seen the girls. He was completely puzzled by the question. Although he had heard some crying, he denied seeing anything unusual.

Throughout the rest of the night, I was kept awake by the distant sound of sobbing rising through the darkness periodically. The next day, I wandered the campground searching for any sign of other campers.

Later, I learned that Gaviota State Park is comprised of land that once belonged to Miguel Cordero (1795-1851) and his family. A native of Santa Barbara, Miguel had worked many years as majordomo at Mission La Purisima, which lay several miles north of Gaviota. In

1833, in exchange for his loyal service, he was given a land grant and a wagonload of supplies with which he and his family would establish their own ranch. It is known that Miguel built a home at Gaviota Creek. Through a Cordero family Web site that includes extensive genealogy, I learned that Miguel had many children. His daughters Maria Natividad and Maria Teresa, who both lived at the Gaviota Creek house, were born six years apart, but there is no record of their deaths.

LAS CRUCES ADOBE RUINS

San Julian Road, off Highway 101 near Gaviota State Park
Gaviota Pass 93117

From 1850 to the mid-1880s, a large settlement stood at this site comprised of several adobe buildings, including a barn, stage station, store, saloon, restaurant, hotel, blacksmith shop, and brothel. Established to serve stagecoach travelers and local ranchers, the settlement was erected on ground sacred to local Indians. Their revered ancestors were buried there after a fierce battle with Spanish soldiers around 1802. When Spanish priests moved into the area in the 1820s, they encountered more than 100 graves marked with Indian totems, seashells, and banners. With reverence and respect, the priests placed crosses over many of the graves creating an icon that gave the place the name Las Cruces (the Crosses). After the American annexation of California in 1846, Yankee settlers entered the region and established cattle and sheep ranches. In 1850, the crosses were removed and the ground was cleared for construction of the stage station and other buildings. Today, little remains of Las Cruces except adobe rubble from the barn, hotel, bar, and brothel. The graves of hundreds of Indians remain unmarked under weeds and adobe rubble.

It is said that Las Cruces is haunted by the spirits of those Indians whose graves were desecrated by the construction of the stage station. At night, their spirits walk the hollowed ground. They appear as light anomalies on film and in digital images. Sensitives are aware of masses of thick air moving slowly about the site on windless nights.

Spirits of the Indians are joined by the ghosts of two prostitutes who were strangled by a customer and a man who died in a gunfight. The apparitions of the two women have been seen standing inside the crumbling adobe walls. They appear to be unaware that the saloon in which they once worked is nothing more than a ruin. A psychic who visited Las Cruces reported that she saw a tall man standing in the center of the ruins. Wearing a black, knee-length coat and a wide brim hat, he resembled a gunfighter. The last time I visited the site I found them surrounded by a fence. Ghost hunters may get close enough to perform EVP surveillance and take pictures of the light anomalies that are so frequently encountered there. Many sensitives who visit Las Cruces detect Indian spirits wandering the grounds far beyond the fence.

GHOST OF THE INN KEEPER

Brothers' Restaurant at Mattei's Tavern
2350 Railroad Avenue
Los Olivos 93441
805-688-4820
www.matteistavern.com

Nearly 150 years after Mattei's Tavern opened, the establishment is still an iconic destination for travelers. Swiss immigrant Felix Mattei (1847-1930) started with a small tavern and inn in 1866 and added to it through the years. Today, Mattei's Tavern no longer offers guest rooms, but its historic dining room and bar present visitors with a chance to savor the essence of the 19th century in this historic little town. There is also a good chance of meeting up with the ghost of Felix Mattei or one of the other spirits that haunt the place.

Opened as the Central Hotel, the tavern served a stage line that ran between Santa Barbara to Los Alamos. Stage traffic diminished in the early 1880s when narrow-gauge train connected Avila Beach to Los Olivos. The tracks ended near the tavern leaving a gap in service to the next rail head in Santa Barbara. Passengers heading south disembarked, spent the night at Mattei's inn, and then traveled by stagecoach to Santa Barbara. To accommodate weary travelers, Felix opened a bar over the objections of his wife. A vocal member of the Women's Temperance Union, Lucy Mattei forced Felix to construct a separate building to house the bar because she could not tolerate a drinking establishment attached to her home and place of business.

Today, the bar room is still connected to the original tavern. In 1891, it was used as a temporary jail by the sheriff. He held two criminals there awaiting transportation to Santa Barbara. While waiting for a wagon and team of horses to arrive, an angry mob stormed the bar with the intention of hanging the men. Upon breaking in and overtaking the deputy, the mob found that the criminals had escaped by dressing in women's clothes.

The bar room was once the scene of wild parties and high-stakes poker games in which cattle, land, money, and cars changed hands. Fred Mattei, one of Felix's sons, kept the games going until his death in 1962. In the 1930s and 1940s, the secluded tavern was a popular getaway for Hollywood stars such as Clark Gable, Gary Cooper, Carol Lombard, and George Raft.

The apparition most often sited at the tavern is that of a bearded, elderly man. It is believed by many that this is the ghost of Felix Mattei. A portrait of Felix, painted by his son Clarence hangs over the fireplace in the bar. Ghost hunters should look at it immediately upon arrival and, during the visit, watch for an apparition that resembles Felix.

Psychics have detected the presence of a woman dressed in a white gown. At times, she appears standing by the front door and creates the impression that she is depressed or sad. It is believed she committed suicide at the inn around 1900 by drinking poison.

Other ghostly activity includes unexplained shadows on the walls, intense cold spots, vague apparitions in various locations, and the movement of glasses and silverware on the tables. In the former card room, sensitives hear the hum of male conversation, clink of bottles touching the edge of a glass, and detect the odor of cigars.

While visiting Mattei's Tavern, ghost hunters might consider visiting the region's wineries. Known as the "other wine country," the Santa Barbara wine growing region has more than 100 wineries surrounded by 24,000 acres of spectacular vineyards.

PHANTOM COACH

Mission Drive between Santa Ynez and Solvang
Solvang 93441

A phantom carriage pulled by four black horses has been spotted on Mission Drive, between Santa Ynez and Solvang, and on other roads in the area. From a distance, the phantom appears as black fog, cigar-shaped, streaming over the ground. As the carriage and horses pass, witnesses can see the details of the figures. The phantom carriage has been described as large, black, without a roof, and moving silently on huge spoked wheels. Traveling at an astonishing speed, the horses and carriage pass without a sound. A ghostly man, sporting a tall hat, sits on the driver's bench with a whip in his hand. Some reports mention an elderly woman sitting in the back seat of the carriage. As the phantom passes, details fade and the image, once again, resembles black fog.

The phantom carriage may appear any time between twilight and 3:00 A.M., moving in either direction of Mission Road. It also appears on Alamo Pintado Road between Los Olivos and Solvang and on Baseline Road near Oak Hill Memorial Cemetery. Phantoms such as this are common in England, Ireland, and the eastern United States. A similar phantom appears in Los Angeles at the intersection of Lookout Mountain Avenue and Laurel Canyon Boulevard. In Ireland, it is said that the devil is the driver and his carriage carries away the soul of someone who has just died. In the Santa Ynez region, wealthy ranchers once traveled in large open carriages. These conveyances are quite different from a hearse used for a funeral procession.

The phantom carriage of Santa Ynez is probably a variant of an environmental imprint. Writer and ghost researcher Richard Senate has suggested that this apparition may be a glimpse of something real from a distant era. Its image intrudes on our time period. Usually, phantoms don't move over long distances, although I have seen many black, elongated clouds or fogs move along a street faster than nearby cars. The possibility should be considered that the driver is a ghost who died while driving his team of four black horses.

ANDERSEN'S SPLIT PEA SOUP

376 Avenue of the Flags
Buellton 93427
805-688-5581
www.peasoupandersens.net

Opened in 1924 by Danish immigrants Anton and Juliette Andersen, this restaurant has a well-deserved reputation for serving the best pea soup in the world. The tiny original restaurant was an immediate success thanks to a recipe Juliette brought from Denmark. Since opening, renovations and expansions of the restaurant and an inn enabled the Andersens to keep pace with a growing patronage, composed largely of repeat customers, who turned off nearby Highway 101 for soup that could not be found elsewhere.

Several ghost hunters and psychics have visited the place searching for the ghosts of the original owners. There are numerous reports of unexplained music, flickering lights, the sound of moving furniture that is later found to be untouched, and doors opening and closing by unseen hands. Much of this paranormal activity occurs in rooms that were once the living quarters of Anton and Juliette. R. T. Buell, who once owned and operated a ranch at the site of the present restaurant, may create some of the ghostly activity found here. Buell died in 1905 and was buried in the family graveyard, which is now covered by the restaurant's parking lot. It has been reported that all bodies were removed for reburial elsewhere, but remnants of a Buell family member may remain at the site, a bit disturbed by traffic over his resting place.

GHOSTS OF THE TRAGIC MISSION

Mission La Purisima Concepcion
2295 Purisima Road
Lompoc 93436
805-733-3713

The name of this Spanish mission commemorates a divine event but its history, one of misery and disaster, has created many ghosts. Constructed of mud plaster in 1787, the original building literally dissolved during the rainy season, leaving its 920 inhabitants without a proper church or the necessary living quarters, shops, kitchens, and storage rooms typical of the California missions. In 1802, a new mission was completed. Two years later, Father Payeras arrived to take control of 1,522 Indian converts called neophytes. Days after his arrival outbreaks of measles and smallpox exploded, killing more than 500 neophytes between 1804 and 1807. On December 12, 1812, a massive earthquake and several aftershocks damaged the buildings severely. Fallen roofs exposed the adobe bricks to rain, allowing them to dissolve. A few weeks later, a small dam broke, flooding the mission ground and completing the destruction of the church.

Seeking safer ground, Father Payeras moved the mission four miles north and constructed the new buildings in a long line, rather than the traditional quadrangle, to facilitate evacuation if earthquakes or floods struck again. Neither of these occurred, but the new mission was also the scene of many terrible events. In 1818, a fire swept through several

La Purisima Concepcion, a remote Spanish mission, was the scene of several tragedies that have left numerous ghosts to wander the grounds.

of the buildings, killing some of the Indian women and children. In 1824, a year after the death of Father Payeras, several mission Indians revolted against harsh treatment. They drove Father Ordaz and the soldiers from the mission, barricaded themselves in the church, and held out for a month before a regiment arrived from Monterey. In the ensuing battle, six soldiers and 17 Indians were killed. Seven of the captured Indians were executed in front of the church.

The Mission La Purisima Concepcion never recovered from the conflict between the Indians and the church fathers. By 1834, after another smallpox epidemic, most of the Indians had departed. Ten years later, the buildings were nothing more than ruins. Livestock wandered through the old church, trampling the grave of Father Payeras, whose body was laid to rest beneath the altar of the church.

With such a tumultuous history, it isn't any wonder the mission is haunted. Late in the 19th century, stories began circulating about a mounted ghost riding across the mission grounds and the appearance of the ghost of Don Vicente, who was reportedly murdered in the kitchen. Tales of ghosts of bandits who used the ruins as a hideout and robed figures resembling mission fathers may have been told to keep squatters away. More recently, though, ghost hunters and psychics have discovered the restored mission is full of ghosts.

In the old church, the sounds of mission-era music have been heard. Visitors have reported the loud, lyrical sounds of guitars and flutes and occasionally drums. The muted Spanish words, sung by male voices, echo throughout the church. When the music fades away, brief sound bursts of a male voice saying mass have been heard. These audio phenomena cannot be attributed to the mission's speaker system. Many people, including ghost hunters, have heard the music and mass recitals when the mission's sound system was turned off or not working. Spectral sounds of bells, footsteps, and voices have been heard in almost every room of the mission and in the graveyard at the west end of the church.

Transparent robed figures have been spotted walking around the mission grounds and inside many of the rooms. One of these is believed to be Father Mariano Payeras. He may not be at peace because only half of his body occupies his grave beneath the mission's altar. For an inexplicable reason, the lower half is buried at Mission Santa Barbara.

The ghost of a gardener has been spotted tending the flower

gardens. When approached, this spirit simply vanishes. Images and sounds of little children have been experienced in the church. During restoration in the 1930s, hundreds of skeletons of children, victims of smallpox and measles, were discovered under the church floor.

GHOSTS OF THE GETAWAY INN

Santa Maria Inn
801 South Broadway
Santa Maria 93454
800-462-4276
www.santamariainn.com

Located 40 miles north of Santa Barbara, on the historic El Camino Real, the Santa Maria Inn has served as a getaway for Hollywood stars, CEOs, famous writers, rock stars, ambassadors, and even presidents since it opened in 1917. The major stars of Cecil B. DeMille's 1923 classic *The Ten Commandants* stayed at the inn while filming Egyptian scenes in the Guadalupe sand dunes. In the 1930s and 1940s, guests from Hollywood destined for William Randolph Hearst's castle in San Simeon disembarked from the train at Santa Maria station and spent a night at the inn before completing their exciting journey in Hearst's limousines. In 2006, when *Pirates of the Caribbean: World's End* was filmed in the same sand dunes, Johnny Depp stayed at the inn.

The Santa Maria Inn was the great dream of Frank McCoy (1872-1949) who came to the area in 1904 to work at the Union Sugar plant. Industrious and dedicated to his dream of owning an inn, Frank saved his money for years, and after he retired, he began building a rustic hotel in 1915. Early success enabled him to upgrade the accommodations, establish an award-winning rose garden, and create one of the best inns on California's central coast. Several rounds of renovations done over the past 90 years have created the spectacular modern structure that offers travelers everything they could want, including a beautiful wine cellar.

Long after his death, Frank seems pleased with the place. His ghost has been seen at several locations inside the inn and in the gardens. Standing tall and slim, he appears in a three-piece suit and wire-rimmed glasses.

Ghosts inhabit several of the rooms. The ghost of silent film star Rudolph Valentino may haunt room 210. His spirit may be responsible for the male presence that guests encounter. The partial apparition has appeared standing at the foot of the bed and in the doorway to the bathroom. This ghost also creates a knocking sound coming from inside the walls, cold spots, and lights that turn on and off.

In room 103, the bathroom door swings open slowly and then slams shut. Outside the door, the sound of someone pacing back and forth has awakened guests. When they open the door to investigate, no one is seen in the hallway. In room 216, curtains move without breezes from an open window or the air-conditioning vent. Intense cold spots move about room 144. In this room, a psychic who was investigating spirits at the inn witnessed a bar of soap move horizontally across the bathroom and drop at his feet as he stood in the shower.

The apparition of a man dressed in a dark blue uniform has been spotted at several locations within the inn. He appears most frequently on an outside staircase overlooking the garden. It is rumored this is the ghost of a merchant marine officer who murdered his mistress at the inn.

In 1989, writer and ghost investigator Richard Senate and gifted psychic Debbie Christensen performed a séance at the hotel and contacted the spirit of a young woman whose nickname was Peppy. This spirit was awaiting a Hearst limousine for a ride to the famed Casa Encantada at San Simeon. There are indications, however, that Peppy may have died of a drug overdose before the limo arrived.

GHOST OF THE ONE-LEGGED MAN

Far Western Tavern
899 Guadalupe Street
Guadalupe 93434
805-343-2211

Opened in 1958 by Clarence and Rosalie Minetti, the popular

restaurant and bar has served local cowboys and farmers for more than 50 years. The building was constructed some time before 1930, however, giving the place a long and vague history that has fostered rumors of colorful characters and bizarre occurrences.

In 1932, the two-story building was used as a cheap hotel for traveling salesmen and produce merchants. Mr. Franchoneti, a fertilizer salesman, was a hotel regular. He frequented the hotel because it was situated in the heart of the Santa Maria agricultural district midway between Santa Barbara and San Luis Obispo. The seedy brothels of Guadalupe might have offered some attraction as well. When he retired, Franchoneti returned to the hotel as a permanent resident. Handicapped by the loss of a leg in World War I, he used an artificial limb, which enabled him to walk short distances. When he moved about his second-floor room, the prosthesis created a characteristic gait that generated a sound often described as a peg leg hitting the floor.

One night in 1937, a fire swept through the building, filling the second floor with smoke. Awakened by the heat and blinded by the smoke, Franchoneti was unable to find and attach his prosthesis. Overcome by the flames, he died in his room.

The building sat vacant for several years before repairs and renovations, and dissipation of the smell of charred wood, made the place habitable. In 1958, after the Minetti's opened the tavern, patrons lounging in the bar late at night heard someone walking around on the second floor with a thumping sound. Old timers who once knew Franchoneti immediately recognized the sound and surmised that the old man's ghost was still walking around his former room.

The thumping sound of a crude prosthesis hitting the floor can be heard through the ceiling of the ground-floor dining room. The old man's apparition has been spotted on the second floor, in the back room of the tavern, and on the staircase. In Franchoneti's former room, an intense cold spot has been located, which is believed to be the place where the unfortunate man's ashes were found.

An organization called Central Coast Paranormal Investigators (CCPI) has investigated the tavern, searching for Franchoneti's ghost and other spirits that may occupy the bar. The place is known for light anomalies, so if you stop by for dinner, bring your camera.

GHOST OF THE LITTLE GIRL

Rose Victorian Inn
789 Valley Road
Arroyo Grande 93420
805-481-5566

Little Alice loves to run up and down the staircase and spend afternoons in the tower room of the Victorian mansion on Valley Road. She also likes to play tug of war with pillows and blankets, project her voice through the speakers of the house's music system, and play with cats. Alice loves to play tricks on the employees who work in the inn by hiding objects, shaking the beds and scaring the people in them, and creating strange lights. Decked out in her mid-calf-length dress and apron, and with her hair in pigtails, Alice has the run of the house and plenty of time to enjoy the place. She doesn't have chores to do or school to attend because she is dead.

Those who have seen Alice estimate her to be nine years old. She appears happy, often displaying a charming smile that suggests she is completely oblivious to the fact that she is dead. The cause and date of her death is uncertain. It has been suggested that she died after falling out of the window, from an allergic reaction to a bee sting, or from pneumonia or scarlet fever. In researching the genealogy of the two families that occupied the home, I was unable to discover any information about the death of a girl named Alice.

My research of this house indicates that the name of this ghost was not derived from any historical record. A psychic who visited the house claims that when she asked the ghost to say her name, the reply was "Alice."

The builder of the house, Charles Pitkin moved to California from Hartford, Connecticut, on February 1, 1876, a few years after the death of his wife, Jane Ann Hastings. Leaving his adult sons, Albert, Howard, and William, in Hartford, Charles moved west alone and settled in Arroyo Grande. In 1889, at the age of 59, he married Julia Louis Goodwin (1828-1896). It is likely that he built the grand Victorian mansion, which is now called the Crystal Rose Inn, as a wedding gift for his new bride. The couple moved into the house in 1890, and Charles died not long after on February 21, 1892. His funeral was staged in the parlor. There is no record of any children born to Charles and Julia Pitkins in California.

In 1905, Edgar and Abigail Conrow purchased the Pitkin house and moved in with their four children, Mary West, Clayton, Gwyneth, and Albert. The youngest, Albert, was born in the house on July 10, 1906. The Conrows stayed in the house until 1957. While the dates of death for the boys and Mary can be found in historical records (Albert in 1984, Clayton in 1975, and Mary in 1952), there is little information about Gwyneth. Mary lived in the house until her death. Thus, it is possible she gave birth to a daughter in the mansion sometime between 1907 and 1930. The child may have died at an early age.

It is also possible that Gwyneth may be the ghost known as "Alice." The ghost's age, as perceived or estimated by psychics, does not conform well to Gwyneth's history, however. She was born in 1894, some distance from Arroyo Grande, and arrived by train in 1905 at the age of 11. If she died at the age of nine, the death would have occurred somewhere other than the Valley Road mansion.

Ghost hunters should call out Conrow family names, especially Gwyneth, when performing EVP sweeps in the mansion. If the ghost was a member of the Conrow family, the familiar names should evoke a clear reply from playful Alice.

GHOST OF THE FACELESS PADRE

Mission San Luis Obispo de Tolosa
751 Palm Street
San Luis Obispo 93405
805-781-8220
www.missionsanluisobispo.org

The beautiful Mission San Luis Obispo de Tolosa sits in the heart of a modern town, between the El Camino Real and the tiny San Luis Obispo Creek, and hardly shows its age. Indeed, visitors unfamiliar with California's mission history might guess it to be a charming architectural remnant from the mid-20th century. But the red tile roof, bell niches in the facade, and long colonnade are typical of 18th-century Spanish ecclesiastical construction dictated, in part, by available building materials and the skill of Native Americans pressed into service to make bricks, tiles, or create decorative paint embellishments. Built in 1793 and restored in 1933, the mission is one of the best preserved in the state and offers modern visitors the same peaceful ambience sought by Spanish soldiers, explorers, travelers, and Indian converts throughout the first half of the 19th century. The courtyard garden remains as a monument to neophytes and priests who lived and worked at the mission.

As peaceful as the mission appears today, it was not always a safe haven. In 1824, an Indian uprising occurred at several central coast missions. Driven from their quarters by rampaging renegades, several neophytes and a monk barricaded themselves in the church. The attackers burned the wooden doors and entered the church, killing those who had taken refuge there. The bodies of the dead were buried in the mission cemetery, but the spirit of one victim still walks the grounds.

The apparition of a short, slim man was first reported in 1935, soon after completion of a major restoration. Wearing a brown robe

In 1824, Mission San Luis Obispo de Tolosa was the site of an Indian uprising. Today, a peaceful community surrounds it but ghosts remain.

and a wide braided sash, the apparition has been identified as that of a monk. Some witnesses have reported seeing amazing details, such as rosary beards that hang from a hand hidden by long sleeves and a metal cross attached to the sash. A large hood, or cowl, covers the monk's head. A priest who encountered this lifelike apparition in the garden reported that he pulled the cowl from the ghost's head. The garment did not feel anything like real cloth, but the cowl fell away from the ghost's head revealing that he had no face. Perhaps the ghost monk's face had been disfigured in the fire and vicious attack of the Indians.

It is said that the ghost monk appears in the mission garden on nights when the moon is full. However, the partial apparitions of robed figures have been spotted at several locations around the mission in broad daylight. Inside the church, disembodied chants spoken in Spanish have been heard.

Other places to hunt ghosts:

TAHITIAN VILLAGE

31 Tah Vil Drive
Lompoc 93436
805-735-7482

Many locals believe this apartment complex was built over a Chumash Indian burial ground. There is no official report of artifacts or graves unearthed during construction, but many apartment dwellers have experienced disembodied voices speaking in a language that is unlike anything they've ever heard. Some residents have reported waking in the morning and finding scratches on their faces or backs.

LA PLACITA MARKET

515 Orchard Road
Nipomo 93444
805-929-4433

Patronized by locals for decades, La Placita Market is the type of "mom and pop" store that has disappeared from big cities. Central Coast Paranormal Investigators has visited the market and captured some interesting orbs in the storage room. Light anomalies are common in some environments, but when linked to the kind of bizarre experiences some employees have had, they may represent spirit energy.

SANTA MARIA CEMETERY

730 East Stowell Road
Santa Maria 93454
805-925-4595

Several of the region's pioneers are buried at the Santa Maria Cemetery. Look for old graves that have been damaged by weather, vandals, or the passage of time. Also, look for the graves of children. These are good locations for EVP.

MADONNA INN

100 Madonna Road
San Luis Obispo 93405
805-543-3000
www.madonnainn.com

This unique inn is known throughout the United States for its elaborate restrooms and bizarre, custom-designed décor. Furnishings range from lurid and sexy to something reminiscent of a jungle, the rooms have names that give guests a clue to what lies ahead. If you are ready for an adventure, try the Jungle Rock, Love Nest, Safari Room, or Caveman. After a stellar opening in 1958 and a meteoric rise to fame, the inn's original rooms were destroyed by fire in 1966. Rebuilt and expanded to 109 rooms, Alex Madonna told the *New York Times* that he wanted people to "come in with a smile and leave with a smile." Will a ghostly encounter be part of the Madonna Inn experience?

BURGER KING

1153 North H Street
Lompoc 93436
805-736-8111

There are reports of a ghost in the women's restroom that resembles a white, pale apparition of a boy who, when alive, was known as Sonny. The victim of a suicide by hanging, the boy now creates a banging sound heard by workers throughout the store as they close the place at night. No one has ventured into the restroom to check on the source of the noise, but a store employee told me that it sounds as if the stall door is being slammed against the walls.

CHAPTER 6

The Inland Missions and Towns

In the final decades of the 18th century, as Spanish explorers and missionaries moved northward, they found no route that would enable them to stay within view of the ocean. At San Luis Obispo, rolling hills and plains, however, offered relatively easy travel for commanders on horseback and the soldiers and *padres* who walked. Giving up their hope of establishing a chain of missions from San Diego to San Francisco, each within a short distance of an ocean port for supply ships, the Spanish were impressed by the vast, fertile lands that lay along the eastern slope of the rugged coastal mountains. These lands offered water, building materials, a hospitable year-round climate, and tribes of Indians that could be drawn to the Spanish missions as Catholic converts and indentured laborers. The inland route northward also offered relatively easy travel between Los Angles, Monterey, and the San Francisco Bay Area and fostered development of a dusty path that became El Camino Real (Royal Highway), which is still in use today. The inland route also led to the development of several Spanish and Mexican settlements such as San Juan Bautista and Paso Robles that are popular venues for ghost hunting. The chain of inland missions, including San Miguel, San Antonio de Padua, and Soledad, each have tragic stories of fatal epidemics and horrific crimes that have created restless spirits.

CHARLOTTE'S GHOST

Adelaida Cemetery
Chimney Rock Road near Klau Mine Road
Adelaida 92301

Opened in 1878 as a final resting place for the region's sheep ranchers and mercury mine workers, and intended by founder Wesley Burnett as a peaceful oasis for the dearly departed, Adelaida Cemetery has become known as one of the most terrifying graveyards in California. I've accumulated a large collection of reports from visitors detailing experiences ranging from a little freaky to nearly disabling fear and anxiety. Many who visit the place during the hours when its ghosts are most active find that they can't even get out of their cars. Facing the graveyard inside a parked car, people have reported sudden strong winds buffeting their cars, dark clouds suddenly engulfing them, red eyes staring at them from inside the graveyard, and bizarre sounds, including whistles, screams, chanting, and growling. Things can be even more frightening inside the graveyard.

During daylight hours, rattlesnakes are the greatest danger. Ghost hunters exercise extreme caution in the spring and summer. Unseen obstacles such as broken headstones and roots protruding above ground can also be a hazard. Some ghost hunters have reported that an evil spirit walks the graveyard at night. Preceded by the appearance

The headstones of Charlotte Sitton and others who died young have been the focus of several paranormal investigations at Adelaida Cemetery.

of beady red eyes piercing the darkness, the spirit brushes past people as if it is trying to scare visitors away. Sometimes, this spirit groans and growls. A few visitors claim that a strong, invisible entity has pushed them to the ground. At several gravesites, sensitive visitors are suddenly overcome with fear and intense sadness. At almost any location in the graveyard, orbs show up in photographs and EAP are easily captured on recording devices.

All of this is in sharp contrast to the history of the most active ghost at Adelaida Cemetery, Charlotte Sitton. Wife of Frank Sitton, Charlotte died on December 19, 1890, at the age of 19. Her death by suicide occurred after several months of depression following the deaths of her children from diphtheria. Charlotte's engraved headstone is tilted but still legible. It stands a short distance from graves believed to be those of her children. These graves are marked with small stones that are so badly weathered the names cannot be read. Every Friday, between 10:00 P.M. and midnight, Charlotte's ghost approaches these graves. Her apparition has been described variously as a greenish glow hovering over the headstones to a transparent but fully developed female image complete with a bouquet of flowers in her hand. Some witnesses claim that Charlotte appeared wearing a pink dress, hence the moniker, the Pink Lady of Adelaida. Charlotte's ghost has frightened numerous people, but she is not threatening. It is likely her appearance late at night, surrounded by the spooky atmosphere of the graveyard, moves some people beyond their emotional limit, resulting in a fear reaction instead of something more appropriate. Sensitive ghost hunters who have had a close encounter with Charlotte's ghost believe she is remorseful for her suicide and deeply misses her children.

Charlotte may move beyond the confines of the graveyard. Reports have been posted on the Internet of a lady in a long white dress that walks alongside Chimney Rock Road. As cars approach, she does not wave them down. After passing the woman, drivers glance in their rear-view mirror only to find the road behind them completely empty.

If you plan to visit this cemetery, take a trustworthy companion and equipment with reliable flashlights. Some ghost hunters also recommend holy water, a cross, and a Bible for protection against the evil spirits that may haunt this place.

GHOST OF THE NIGHT CLERK

Paso Robles Inn
1103 Spring Street
Paso Robles 93446
805-238-2660
www.pasoroblesinn.com

Minutes before 9:00 P.M. on December 12, 1940, night clerk J. E. Emsley made his customary rounds of the corridors of the Paso Robles Inn. Always a formality more than anything else, the walk reassured Emsley that the inn's 200 guests were settled for the night and the corridors were clear of discarded room-service trays and other items. On this night, however, Emsley turned a corner on the second floor and smelled something burning. Looking about, he discovered discolored paint on the ceiling. A moment later, the corridor filled with smoke.

Fearing a major disaster was about to occur, Emsley rushed downstairs, dashed behind the clerk's desk, pulled the fire alarm at 9:05 P.M., and dropped dead. Hearing the alarm, hotel manager Eugene Santelman ran from his office and ushered the guests out of the building as the fire department arrived. It was some time later that Emsley's lifeless body, concealed by the clerk's desk, was discovered.

Built in 1891 with more than one million bricks, the Paso Robles Inn was believed to be fireproof. It is considered one of the finest resorts on the central coast and offers guests a large swimming pool, nine-hole golf course, magnificent seven-acre garden, library, hot-springs bathhouse, and all the personal services well-heeled travelers could desire. With so much to offer, it isn't any wonder that notables such as Pres. Theodore Roosevelt, boxing champ Jack Dempsey, and several movie stars frequented the establishment.

By 1942, the Paso Robles Inn was completely rebuilt with the exception of the ballroom. Suffering only smoke damage, the ballroom was restored and stands today as part of the modern inn. When doors opened in late 1942, many of the staff returned to work, including J. E. Emlsey. His ghost walks the corridors still looking for signs of a fire or anything else that might be a threat to the hotel. Fixated on the alarm he sounded, Emsley's ghost makes 911 calls at about the same time, 9:05 P.M. Many of these calls come from room 1007. Emsley also calls the front desk from rooms not occupied by living guests. Several entries in the inn's log made by employees indicate a very active and vigilant ghost.

Aside from J. E. Emsley, a female ghost walks the gardens and courtyard. This may be the Lady in White that has been sighted since the 1950s. Some witnesses have reported that she appears completely lifelike, greeting them and then vanishing before their eyes. One staff member told me this ghost has been named Blanche by the staff. A woman of that name worked at the inn for more than 40 years before she died.

CURSE OF THE LITTLE BASTARD

James Dean Death Site
Highway 46 at Highway 41
Jack Ranch Café
19215 East Highway 46
Shandon 93446
805-238-5652

James Byron Dean's tragic death at the age of 24 sent shock waves through Hollywood and brought many of his fans to tears. More famous than Brad Pitt, the surly, brooding actor was often compared to Marlon Brando. His brilliant performances in *East of Eden* (1955), *Giant* (released in 1956), and, his signature film, *Rebel without a Cause* (1955) brought him superstar status. The rebellious persona he displayed on screen and off, and his sex appeal, has sustained his position as a Hollywood icon 50 years after his death. He won the Oscar for best actor posthumously, and it seems he continued his rebel-without-a-cause recklessness after his death by creating a curse.

On September 30, 1955, Dean was traveling west on Highway 46 with his mechanic, Rolf Wütherich. His destination was Salinas, where he intended to race his Porsche 550 Spyder, nicknamed the Little Bastard. As they neared the interaction with Highway 41, near

Cholame, 23-year-old Donald Turnupseed approached them from the opposite direction. Maneuvering to take a sharp right turn onto the highway, Turnupseed crossed the centerline and collided head-on with Dean's Spyder. Dean survived the impact but died upon arrival at Paso Robles Memorial Hospital. Wütherich was thrown from the car but suffered only a broken jaw and other nonfatal injuries. Turnupseed sustained only minor injuries.

Today, a memorial stands alongside Highway 46 about 900 yards from the actual site of the accident. The nearby Jack Ranch Café has also become a shrine to James Dean. After the accident, the damaged Spyder was stored for a short time in a shed next to the café. Growing notoriety surrounding the death of the young actor added a mystique to the place, and the café filled its walls with poster's from Dean's movies and other memorabilia. For many years, stories circulated about headlights approaching the café at night and then disappearing without signs of a car or truck pulling into the parking area. Today, the café has been replaced by a convenience store, but it may be a good place to connect with locals who can tell some bizarre stories about Dean's accident and the curse he may have placed on his Porsche Spyder.

Although James Dean loved his Porsche Spyder, he may have cursed the wrecked vehicle. Several accidents have befallen those who handled the wrecked car or used salvaged parts. Two rear tires, undamaged by the accident, later blew up simultaneously, causing the new owner's car to career off the road. On at least five occasions, when the car was being transported on flatbed trucks, safety chains gave way, causing serious injuries. In one instance, the Porsche slid off the flatbed and crushed the driver who had stopped to inspect his load. Two doctors, Troy McHenry and William Eschrid purchased engine and drive train parts, installed them in their cars, and entered the same race. McHenry was killed when his car spun out and crashed into a tree. Eschrid was seriously injured when his vehicle rolled over.

In the late 1950s, the California Highway Patrol (CHP) purchased the shell of Dean's car with the intention of using it in accident prevention displays. While stored in a CHP garage, a fire swept through the place destroying everything except the Spyder. Eventually, the car was purchased by George Barris. While it was being transported to his auto customizing shop, it disappeared. A few parts show up now and again, but the whereabouts of James Dean's cursed Little Bastard remains unknown.

The series of tragic accidents surrounding the Little Bastard invited speculation that Dean himself cursed the car as he lay dying in the ambulance en route to the hospital. It is possible the curse arose from some other source. On September 23, 1955, Dean had a chance encounter with actor Alec Guinness outside of a Hollywood restaurant. As the conversation rolled around to common interests, Dean asked Guinness to look at his car. Looking over the sporty vehicle, Guinness said, "If you get in that car, you will be found dead in it by this time next week." James Dean died seven days later.

GHOSTS OF THE MURDERED TRAVELERS

Los Coches Rancho Adobe
Arroyo Seco Road at Highway 101
Monterey County
Near Soledad 93960

Built in 1843, this historic rancho and stagecoach depot now stand in ruins awaiting donations that would restore it to its former grandeur. The building was once the hub of the Soberanes rancho, which stood on a Mexican land grant of 8,990 acres. Today, the wood and adobe structure is situated on 10 acres donated to the state in 1958. Ghosts of the Soberanes and Richardson families, and travelers on the Bixby Overland Stage that connected Los Angeles and San Francisco, may walk its halls.

In 1841, Maria Josefa Soberanes received a grant of 8,994 acres from Mexican governor Juan Alvarado principally in homage to her grandfather, Jose Soberanes, who, at the age of 16, served as a soldier in Portola's 1769 expedition that opened California to Spanish settlement. Previous Spanish and Mexican governors had granted huge parcels of land to the Soberanes family, amounting to 115,000 acres. With her Anglo husband of two years, William Brunner Richardson, Josefa, as she was called, built a two-room adobe on the land; it was later expanded to a two-story house covered with wood siding.

With a gift of 300 cattle, the rancho flourished for a few years until Gen. John Charles Fremont and his regiment camped on the property for six months in 1846. Helping themselves to cattle, horses, crops, and water, they left the rancho nearly destitute. The U.S. government has yet to pay a standing bill of $580 for goods that Fremont and his men consumed. After California became an American territory, and then a state, Josefa faced greater financial stresses as she was forced to defend her land title in several legal disputes. To make ends meet, she and her husband opened their home as a stage stop, offering overnight accommodations for travelers and fresh horses for the stages. From 1854 to 1865, when she was finally forced from the land, Josefa may have engaged in a scheme that brought quick wealth to her family. She allegedly murdered travelers who were fresh from the Sierra mining camps, threw their bodies down a well, and buried the gold somewhere on the property. There is no proof that murders were committed at Los Coches, but the small bedrooms on the second floor of the adobe are almost too frightening to enter. Sensitive visitors, including me, can hardly enter these tiny rooms without sensing the horror and dread that still fills them. I got the impression that the entire second floor is filled with unseen spirits who are angry and still suffering a painful death.

Aside from murder victims, the ghosts of outlaws such as Joaquin Murrieta and Three-fingered Jack may haunt the property. These notorious figures did not die on the premises, but they may have been Josefa's accomplices.

Access to the aging adobe is limited, but some sensitive visitors have felt transported back in time to the Mexican Period of California history. One woman fell into a trance and began speaking Spanish, a language she had never studied. Rumors of buried treasure haunt the old rancho, but there is only one documented report of a discovery of valuables. A gold ring was found at the foot of an oak tree after a visitor learned of its location through a trance. It is of interest that water on the property has been declared unsafe for consumption by humans and livestock. A city worker told me that the ground water is badly contaminated. This report left me wondering if the bodies Josefa dumped down the well have somehow contaminated local ground water.

GHOSTS OF THE MASSACRED FAMILY

Mission San Miguel
775 Mission Street
San Miguel 93451
805-467-3256 (gift shop)
805-467-2131 (parish office)
www.missionsanmiguel.org

Most ghost stories associated with California's Spanish missions are shrouded in mystery, blended with myth and legend, and have little in the way of historical record to explain the haunting or identify the ghost. None of this applies to the ghosts of Mission San Miguel. Thanks to the confessions of two murderers and accounts of reliable men who discovered the horrific crime scene, we know most of the details of the mass murder that took place in the mission, including the names of the perpetrators and their victims.

By 1836, the Catholic Church had lost control of the missions and their vast land holdings to the Mexican government. The process of secularization was swift, driving Indians from the missions and

In 1848, several murders occurred inside Mission San Miguel leaving ghosts to walk the grounds searching for help.

opening up valuable lands to a growing number of wealthy ranchers. In 1846, William Reed and his partner Petronilo Rios purchased the deserted and disintegrating Mission San Miguel and a few hundred acres of land for $250. A few years later, Reed opened his mission as an inn for travelers returning to southern California from the Gold Rush country. Offering meals, accommodations, and horses in exchange for gold, Reed accumulated a small fortune, which he claimed he buried on his property.

On the afternoon of December 4, 1848, a band of fugitives arrived at the Reed home. They were led by Joseph Lynch, an army deserter, and Peter Raymond, an escaped murderer from the Gold Rush country town of Murphys. Among the band were two British pirates who had deserted from the warship *Warren* while it was moored in Monterey Bay. A fugitive Indian boy from the Mission Soledad accompanied them. After dinner, while Lynch paid for one night's lodging, he listened to Reed brag about the large amount of money he had made from successful gold miners who had stayed at his inn. The band left the next day and pondered the buried treasure that might be easily stolen. The thought of sacks of gold slowed their pace, and eventually they turned around and returned to the Reed home, arriving at sunset. Pretending they desired another night's lodging, the men were invited into the mission. Within minutes, the carnage began. Lynch struck Reed several times with an axe as the Indian boy stabbed him with a long knife.

The other men went to the kitchen and bedrooms and killed Reed's pregnant wife, Maria Vallejo; his four-year-old son; his brother-in-law, Ramon Vallejo; his midwife, Josefa Olivera; a 15-year-old girl; the visiting grandson of a neighbor; a cook; and an Indian shepherd and his grandchild. Counting the unborn child, 11 died that night. Some of the men drank Reed's wine while they dismembered the bodies.

Almost too drunk to do a thorough search, the murderers ransacked the home, taking all the valuables they found. Then, they dragged all the bodies to the family's living room (now the mission's model room) and piled them one on top of the other. This gruesome process spread blood throughout several rooms and halls.

While the murderers escaped southward to Santa Barbara, mail rider James E. Beckwourth, who left a detailed account of the grizzly scene, discovered the bodies of the massacred family. A posse caught up with the outlaws 15 miles south of Santa Barbara. One outlaw was shot and killed while a second drowned in the surf while attempting an escape. Peter Remer, Joseph Lynch, and Peter Quinn were captured, tried, and executed by firing squad on December 28, 1848.

The details of this mass murder, including the names of the victims and perpetrators, are useful to ghost hunters who perform EVP sweeps at the mission. Ghosts of the murdered family and some of the murderers still walk the rooms of the old mission. Call and response directed at William Reed, Maria Vallejo, or the murderers may evoke startling responses. The apparition of a woman, possibly Maria, known as the Lady in White floats through several rooms of the old mission. Witnesses report that she appears to be desperately searching for something or someone. The transparent apparition of a man dressed in a blue coat drifts down the arcade and through the dining room and kitchen. Accounts dictated by Reed's neighbor indicate that he was often seen sporting his blue pea coat, complete with brass buttons. It should be noted, however, that when apprehended, one of the outlaws was wearing Reed's pea coat.

Inside the rooms of the old mission, sensitive visitors experience sudden, intense fear for no apparent reason. Some are overcome with dread and burst into tears even without prior knowledge of the massacre. A bloody handprint appearing on a wall in the living room is believed to have been made by the wounded William Reed as he ran from his attackers, trying to warn his family. Numerous efforts to wash the print off the wall have failed. It has been covered by thick coats of paint only to reappear months later.

Ghosts of the outlaws may wander the mission grounds searching for the buried gold that inspired their crime. When apprehended, the murderers had only 242 pesos, seven reales in silver, and an ounce of gold. Legend says that Reed's stash of gold, perhaps as much as $200,000 (in 1848 dollars), remains undiscovered on the mission grounds.

Other ghosts spotted at the Mission San Miguel include a robed monk who walks the arcade and partial apparitions of Indians whose remains lay in unmarked graves that may have been desecrated by the paving of Mission Street or other modern structures.

GHOST OF THE HEADLESS HORSEWOMAN

Mission San Antonio de Padua
Mission Road
Jolon 93928
831-385-4478
www.missionsanantoniodepadua.net

Sitting miles from Highway 101, Mission San Antonio de Padua is the most remote of the 21 Spanish missions. Established July 14, 1771, by Father Junipero Serra and named for Saint Anthony, the mission property once had an elaborate irrigation system and gristmill, which contributed significantly to its success. At its peak, in 1827, 1,300 Indians lived at the mission, working to manage 7,000 sheep and 800 horses. Located far to the north of the southern coastal mission, San Antonio was spared the misery of the Indian revolt of 1824. Like other missions, however, many Indians died from imported diseases, including smallpox and cholera. Consequently, a large number of unmarked graves surround San Antonio. Tales of ghosts wearing Indian clothing or the robes of a *padre* are still told by excited visitors.

Archeology students working at the mission have posted reports of their encounters with a candle-carrying priest. This ghost walks an outdoor corridor overlooking the courtyard. Some witnesses have mistaken this ghost, which appears lifelike in the dim light of evening, for one of the living priests working at the mission. When the witness and the apparition come face to face, the image vanishes, leaving nothing but the faint fragrance of a burning candle.

The most fascinating ghost story associated with Mission San Antonio sounds more like an urban legend, but it comes with verification by reliable witnesses. The apparition of a headless woman on a horse has been spotted riding the crest of hills near the mission and at a location within the surrounding military reservation, Ammo Supply Point (ASP). Since her first appearance late in the 19th century, the headless rider has been referred to as Cleora by local Indians.

Legend says that Cleora's husband caught her with a man who was prospecting in the area. Fueled with rage, the husband killed Cleora by cutting off her head. To ensure her misery and shame, he buried her body near the mission and her head at the current site of the ASP. Now her restless, headless spirit rides the countryside in search of her head.

It would be easy to dismiss this story as an Indian legend told to discourage settlement in the region. However, several credible witnesses have reported encounters with Cleora. Soldiers stationed at Fort Hunter-Liggett have filed official reports of the horse and headless rider approaching the ASP. One soldier even said that he drew his weapon and commanded the rider to stop. A mission monk, Brother Timothy, reported that four military policemen swore in his presence that they had witnessed Cleora and chased her in their jeep. Mounted on a fast horse, the ghost escaped into the brush.

Ghost hunters who visit Mission San Antonio might encounter Cleora in front of the mission church at sunrise and sunset.

GHOST OF THE GREAT WRITER

John Steinbeck House
132 Central Avenue
Salinas 93901
831-424-2735
www.steinbeckhouse.com

The spirit of John Steinbeck (1902-1968) must be one of those rare traveling ghosts, because he has appeared on Cannery Row in Monterey; at his home on Sag Harbor, Long Island; and in the Salinas house in which he was born. He lived in the Salinas house until 1919 when he enrolled at Stanford University. With the exception of summer vacations and holidays, Steinbeck never spent much time in the farming community, but, drawing upon the vivid experiences of his youth, he wrote some monumental books about the people and historical conditions and events of the region. His *Grapes of Wrath*, published in 1939, described the horrors of the Great Depression from Oklahoma to California and won the Pulitzer Prize for literature. His book *East of Eden* (1952) was written for his sons, to give them a lasting chronicle of their heritage derived from ranchers of the great

The ghost that haunts the John Steinbeck house in Salinas may be that of the great writer who died in 1968.

Salinas Valley. Seventeen of Steinbeck's books have been adapted into Hollywood films, and in 1944, Steinbeck was honored with an Academy Award nomination for Best Story for Alfred Hitchcock's *Lifeboat.*

In his later years, Steinbeck lived in Sag Harbor, Long Island, but some of his closest friends who I interviewed in 1987 told me that his heart was torn between Salinas and Monterey. In particular, Sparky Enea said that if Steinbeck's ghost was still on the planet, he would first go home to Salinas.

Today, Steinbeck's boyhood home is a shrine for fans of the writer and others who are fascinated with Salinas Valley history. The Valley Guild, a nonprofit organization dedicated to preservation of Steinbeck's home, operates a restaurant and gift shop in the house and conducts tours. Several tour guides have reported paranormal activity, which has been attributed to the great writer. A yellow mist in the shape of a man has appeared in several locations in the house, particularly in the front room near the window facing Central Avenue. Others have actually seen an apparition resembling Steinbeck as he appeared in his final year of life. This ghost moves about, gliding rather than walking, and appears pleased with the condition of the house. The sound of doors opening and closing has also been reported for decades, beginning two years after Steinbeck's death and continues today.

GHOSTS OF THE GREAT MISSION

Mission San Juan Bautista
406 South Second Street
San Juan Bautista 95045
831-623-4528

Standing outside this impressive Spanish mission, visitors don't fully comprehend what they see. The church does appear large, but once you enter the sanctuary, the size of the place is absolutely amazing. Most of California's Spanish missions were constructed long

Mission San Juan Bautista is one of the largest and oldest Spanish missions in California. Ghostly sounds of drums and Spanish-speaking voices are heard throughout the huge structure.

and narrow to conform to building techniques of the late 1700s. The Mission San Juan Bautista (St. John the Baptist) is not only long, from altar to the great doors, but it is also incredibly wide. In fact, in terms of square footage, it is the largest Spanish church constructed in California. Built in 1797 as the fifteenth mission in a chain stretching from San Diego to Sonoma, the structure still has an atmosphere that transports visitors back to the early 1800s. The painted walls have been restored, but the designs and colors are faithful to the original Indian artwork. Looking to the ceiling, I am amazed that local Mutsun Indians, a handful of Spanish soldiers, and a few priests could construct such a building. If you look closely at the floor tiles, you will see the paw prints of animals that walked across the tiles as they dried in the Salinas Valley sun more than 200 years ago. Touches of obscure human history, such as fingerprints in exposed adobe bricks, are everywhere. If you look for them, you may also discover the ghosts of the great mission.

Along the north wall of the mission, a tiny cemetery fills the space between the church and the infamous San Andreas Fault. Dusty and without impressive monuments, the cemetery contains the remains of more than 4,000 people. Most of the residents of this cemetery are Mutsun Indians converted to Christianity by the mission fathers. Nearly all of their graves are unmarked. Some of the graves contain the remains of mission priests, monks, and other clergy.

Some of the sensitive ghost hunters who visit the church and cemetery have been engulfed with spirit activity. Inside the museum, remnants from the early 1800s emit a vibe that includes chants in Spanish, the sound of crude drums and guitars, and hushed conversations. The area now used as a gift shop once housed the Breen family, survivors of the ill-fated Donner Party disaster of 1846. In the church, cold spots are often discovered, orbs show up in photographs, and the audible rush of robed figures moving through the aisles is often heard when no one is moving about.

From a paranormal perspective, the cemetery may be the most active place in the mission complex. Many of the Indians interred there died of imported diseases, including smallpox, cholera, and measles. The last surviving Mutsun, Ascencion Solorzano, died in 1930. Unlike her ancestors, her grave is marked with a red cross and a plaque. The

Ghostly sounds and light anomalies are common experiences for visitors inside the Mission San Juan Bautista.

The tiny cemetery adjacent to the Mission San Juan Bautista contains the remains of more than 4,000 Indians, including the last member of the Mutsun tribe.

mass burial in this cemetery occurred following the last epidemic to strike San Juan Bautista, which took place in 1886 following the arrival of a stagecoach that brought an ill passenger to town. The man disembarked and staggered into the Plaza Hotel. Within 48 hours, smallpox began killing people. In less than two weeks, 300 people were dead from the disease.

After sunset, the cemetery and grounds outside the north wall are good places to collect EVP and snap pictures of light anomalies. Audio recordings often contain chants in Spanish and a language believed to be a Mutsun dialect. Sensitives who walk the cemetery's pathways hear disembodied footsteps on the sand and the high notes of bells.

THE CUTTING HORSE STEAKHOUSE

307 Third Street
San Juan Bautista 95045
831-623-4549

In nearly every building in San Juan Bautista something strange occurs on a regular basis, leading locals to conclude that the place is haunted. My experience in this town suggests that most buildings are haunted, so the locals are probably right when they tell you about ghosts in their homes, shops, parks, or on a particular street corner. The history of the ghosts they talk about may be more myth than fact, but then, most ghosts have a hidden past that is mysterious and implausible. The Cutting Horse Steakhouse has ghosts, fascinating myths and legends, and enough factual history to give credence to the ghost stories that are told by employees and regular customers.

The building stands over a former Mutsun Indian burial ground, a few hundreds yards from the San Andres Fault. Buried bodies, spiritual energy imparted by Mutsun shamans, and electromagnetic energy emanating from the fault may be responsible for much of the paranormal activity that occurs at the Cutting Horse. Thus, bizarre events occur here, including a sink hose that moved by itself, sprayed the owners, and then returned to its wall bracket. Water left in buckets tends to slosh around as if an unseen worker is trying to move it. Women customers using the restroom report a presence crowding

Ghosts of Indians, cowboys, criminals who were hanged at the site, and a little girl named Diana may haunt the Cutting Horse Steakhouse in San Juan Bautista.

the space. At times, the door is held shut by unseen hands, trapping a nervous customer inside the restroom. Apparitions of cowboys have been spotted as they descend the back stairs that once led to the second-floor brothel. The ghosts of criminals who were hanged from the "hanging tree" that once stood nearby often show up leaning against a wall. Strange, unexplained odors are detected in isolated spots throughout the restaurant and saloon. These include sage, sweaty horses, rum, and cigar smoke.

The structure that houses the Cutting Horse stands on the foundation of a two-story hotel built in 1840 of adobe bricks. The St. John's Hotel offered accommodations to stagecoach travelers and new town residents. This building was nearly destroyed by fire in 1867. It was rebuilt with sandstone and reopened as the French Hotel. In 1874, John Murphy constructed a bakery on the adjacent lot. The two buildings were eventually connected, and today, Murphy's Bakery is the third dining room of the Cutting Horse Steakhouse.

During the wild days of the 19th century, several tragic events occured in this composite building. In 1852, Manuel Butron was shot by a crazy man who stormed into the building, pistol in hand.

This young ghost hunter is searching for the apparition of a female murder victim who appears on the stairs of the Cutting Horse Steakhouse.

Butron took a bullet in his chest, and witnesses assumed he would die within the hour. Wasting no time, they dragged the shooter to the town's nearby hanging tree. The shooter was dead within minutes. Miraculously, Butron survived, making the hanging a perversion of justice. Still angry, the shooter's ghost appears at Cutting Horse separated from the site of the hanging tree by a wall.

Several more ghostly figures appear on the property. A young woman, engaged to a local rancher, fell on the back stairs. The unfortunate woman was moving out of her second-floor room and descending the stairs with her luggage. She slipped and landed at the base of the stairs, dying on the spot of a broken neck. Her apparition repeats the descent but vanishes before she falls.

A little girl named Diana died of smallpox in one of the second-floor rooms. It is likely she died during the epidemic of 1886. Described as a five year old with long curly hair, Diana has been reported by children who visit the Cutting Horse with a parent. Sometimes, lights flicker when she walks into a room.

A young woman murdered on the ground floor walks through the Cutting Horse and adjacent buildings. She appears as a skeletal face with long blond hair, but, at times, witnesses have claimed her face to be lifelike. Her images show up in mirrors and on the staircase.

The apparition of an older, buxom woman moves down the stairs in a flurry and sits in the lounge. She appears completely realistic and resembles the madam who ran a brothel on the second floor in the 1930s.

GHOSTS OF THE ACORN GRINDERS

Chitactac Adams Heritage County Park
10001 Watsonville Road
Gilroy 95020
408-323-0107

Walking around this 4.3-acre preserve it is easy to feel transported back in time 200 years or more to an era before Spanish explorers entered the region. Ignoring the modern conveniences that came with development as a county park, sensitive people find the tranquility of this area mesmerizing. Situated at the base of the eastern slope of the Santa Cruz Mountains and bisected by a year-around stream, the

Ohlone Indians who inhabited these grounds did, indeed, have a piece of paradise.

The Ohlones left their mark on the grounds, but they also conformed to nature. Using oblong, granite pestles, they wore little pockets in slabs of rock, some 12 inches deep, and inscribed petroglyphs on boulders that remain, to this day, without interpretation. The rock pockets were used to grind acorns and seeds, which were a diet staple. They can be found all over the park, wherever broad expanses of rock offered a place for a gathering of Indian women to each squat over a hole with a oblong rock for a pestle and a basket of acorns. When I sat on the grinding rocks, I felt the presence of unseen people gathering around me. At these grinding rocks, I, and other sensitives, have detected the unintelligible chatter of woman speaking the Ohlone language. I've also heard the tap and grind of a rock pestle on the edge of the rock pockets.

Climbing down to the edge of the creek, petroglyphs can be found that defy the interpretative skills of anthropologists, including those who are descendents of the Ohlone. Mentally blocking out the quiet babble of the creek, sensitives detect the din of people talking in an unfamiliar language and pungent odors emanating from a source that cannot be found. These sounds and odors may be environmental imprints created by the people who peacefully occupied the place for hundreds of years.

Ghost hunters should find a broad rock with several grinding pockets, lay down on the rock, and meditate, clearing away the auditory clutter of the present era. Listen for the muted sound of rock scrapping against rock and try to notice the nutty fragrance of freshly ground acorns.

GHOST OF THE OLD TOWN

New Almaden Hacienda Cemetery
21350 Almaden Road
Santa Clara County 95120
408-323-1107

In 1824, Mexican pioneers Luis Chabolla and Antonio Sunol, discovered mercury deposits known as cinnabar on the eastern slope of the Santa Cruz Mountains. It wasn't until 1845, however, that a Mexican cavalry captain, Don Andres Castillero, recognized the value of the discovery and filed a formal claim to the crude diggings. With knowledge of modest gold discoveries made in several locations throughout California, Castillero understood that the mercury in cinnabar was an agent essential for extracting gold from quartz and other rock. With the Gold Rush of 1848, the cinnabar claim passed into the hands of the Barron Forbes Company and eventually the Quicksilver Mining Company. Throughout the ensuing 20 years, the size of the mining operation grew to include 700 buildings, three villages, three major mine shafts, a school, company stores, smelting facilities, and two cemeteries. The company's three villages—Spanishtown, Englishtown, and the Hacienda—were established to accommodate three principle ethnic groups. Today, a county park encloses the mines and preserves the village sites and remnants of the factories built to produce mercury for the 19th-century mining operations in California and Nevada. Along Almaden Road, several houses built for mine supervisors and their families are still used private residences. Many of these houses have ghost stories associated with them, but ghost hunters must get permission from residents before entering private property.

Like most mining operations, cinnabar mining was dangerous work. Fires, cave-ins, accidents, and infections from relatively minor injuries filled the graveyard with young people. Among the early

The Casa Grande in Almaden was once the headquarters for the Almaden Quicksilver Mining Company.

dead were numerous children. Despite the beautiful setting modern visitors encounter, life in the villages was hard, often challenged by privation. The medical clinic established by the mining company could do little for children poisoned by mercury-tainted water or born with birth defects.

Almost hidden from view on Bertram Road, the Hacienda Cemetery contains the remains of many Almaden children and their parents. The visible headstones represent only a fraction of the people interred there. Many grave markers made of wood were destroyed by brush fires that swept through the cemetery while others, even stone markers, were washed away by winter floods from nearby Alamitos Creek. When the narrow road that winds past the cemetery was paved in 1928, several graves were covered. Some of the houses constructed nearby may also sit on unmarked graves. Residents may be willing to share stories of strange lights, cold spots, a sense of an unseen presence, and moving objects inside their homes.

The grave of little Jenny Danielson attracts many visitors. She was born December 7, 1886, and died July 27, 1888. Her grief-stricken parents added, "She was blue eyed and very beautiful," to a plaque or supplemental headstone at her gravesite. At this grave, ghost hunters have captured some fascinating EVP. Long periods of sobbing have been recorded. Sensitives also pick up intense emotions that include grief and anger. These paranormal phenomena are environmental imprints, or residuals, created by living people who made frequent visits to Jenny's grave. This is a common finding in cemeteries, particular at the graves of children. Rarely are spirits of the dead present. Instead, visits by grief-stricken parents, made frequently over a long period, create environmental imprints that are durable and easily detected.

Another fascinating grave in the Hacienda Cemetery is that of Richard Bertram's arm. In 1898, at the age of 13, Bertram lost an arm in a hunting accident. By law, the limb had to be buried. The family complied by creating a miniature plot complete with formal headstone and a picket fence. When the rest of Richard Bertram died in 1959, burial was carried out at Oak Hill Cemetery in San Jose. There is an urban legend about Bertram's arm climbing out of the grave in search of the rest of the body, but ghost hunters dismiss it as they have searched the grounds for orbs, EVP, partial apparitions of mourners, and the head and arm that appear to belong to an angry gravedigger and found no evidence of such occurences.

GHOSTS OF A KIND LADY AND THE MINERS

La Floret Restaurant and other historic Almaden buildings
21747 Bertram Road
San Jose 95120
408-997-3458
www.laforetrestaurant.com

The ghost of a kindly lady walks the floors of this popular French restaurant, but she is rarely noticed by eager patrons who come here from nearby Silicon Valley. Sometimes only the swishing sound of her long skirt is heard through the noise of animated conversation. Late in the evening, when the restaurant is nearly empty of patrons and staff move about quietly, sensitive customers catch a glimpse of a woman in clothing typical of the 19th century. She moves through the dining rooms, appearing to float rather than walk. Witnesses told me they could not see the lower half of her skirt or her feet; however, at times, her apparition displays amazing detail. She has curly gray hair, hazel eyes, and alabaster skin. She is short, perhaps five feet tall, and slim. When she reveals her hands, they appear deformed by arthritis.

La Floret Restaurant is housed in a building constructed in 1848 as

The ghost of a former hotel manager walks the floors of the popular La Floret Restaurant in historic Almaden.

a boarding house for miners who worked at the Almaden Quicksilver Mines. Named the Hacienda Hotel, visitors to the mines also rented rooms there while they conducted business with mine supervisors.

When the mining company declared bankruptcy in 1912, only a few retired miners stayed on as boarders. By 1930, all of the boarders were gone and the place was converted to a restaurant called Café del Rio that served local farmers. At the time, the Almaden area was about 15 miles from the heart of San Jose and isolated from the region's visitors and residents by vast orchards and unpaved roads. Café del Rio closed in the 1960s, leaving the building vacant for many years, but explosive growth of San Jose in the 1970s brought it new life. In 1974, Santa Clara County opened Almaden Quicksilver County Park, bringing in visitors and fostering construction of new houses on the site of the old miners' villages. In 1979, the old Hacienda Hotel building underwent another round of renovations and opened as La Floret. Today, La Floret is a popular destination for Silicon Valley locals who want to stay close to home yet feel that they've left town for a few hours of dining in a remarkable historic setting.

I could not locate detailed historical records that might reveal the name of the kindly lady who walks through La Floret. She may have been the manager of the Hacienda Hotel when it served miners or an early owner of Café del Rio. She seems happy with the modern restaurant, however, and does not appear distressed. Local ghost hunters believe that she is not alone. The ghosts of miners have also been seen on the second floor of the restaurant and the balcony. These ghosts are bearded and appear to be wearing dirty clothes. It is likely these fellows died in their rooms at the Hacienda Hotel.

Ghost hunters should also visit the Casa Grande, the imposing brick mansion on Almaden Road. Constructed in 1854 as a residence for the mine manager and offices for supervisory personnel, the building has been used as a live stage theater and a museum. Ghost hunters might also be interested in the historic homes that sit on a narrow strip of land between Almaden Road and Alamitos Creek. Built in the 1840s and 1850s, most of them have a plaque that outlines their history, including the names of people who resided within. All of them are private residences but access might be granted to serious ghost hunters.

BLOOD ALLEY—HIGHWAY 17

Between the Cats Restaurant (near Los Gatos) and Scott's Valley

Highway 17 winds its way from the Santa Clara Valley through the coastal mountains to the beach in Santa Cruz. Travel along this 26-mile route has been treacherous since the days of the first Spanish settlers. They encountered mountain lions and grizzly bears roaming in herds while they traveled on narrow paths, clinging to steep mountainsides that often gave way under their feet. Modern travelers face different hazards that have made the journey between Los Gatos and Santa Cruz even more hazardous than it was in 1790.

Highway 17 passes through stands of majestic redwoods, wooded valleys, fog-shrouded canyons, and pastures dotted with horses, offering magnificent views of the rugged coastal mountains. In good weather, the passage is a beautiful drive, but it is also one of the most dangerous roads in California. Since the highway opened in 1940, more than 200 people have lost their lives in traffic accidents on this treacherous road. The greatest number of fatalities—36—occurred in 1967. Since 1970, Highway 17 has claimed an average of four lives per year. Nonfatal accidents, some with serious injuries, occur everyday. In 1990, 787 collisions were reported.

With the advent of wider shoulders, better lane markings, warning lights on curves, and concrete barriers on the centerline, the road has become safer, but there is little protection against careless drivers and those operating under the influence of alcohol or drugs. It is no surprise that the greatest frequency of accidents occur on Friday and Saturday around 5:00 P.M. April, May, and June are the worst months for fatalities as warmer weather draws inland dwellers to the beaches for sun and surf. Locals use many nicknames for Highway 17, including Blood Alley, and some of its more dangerous sections.

With the large number of deaths that have occurred on Highway 17, it isn't any wonder that many spirits have not left the scene of their fatal accidents. At sharp turns, startled drivers have heard the sounds of screeching tires and metal as cars collided, yet no accident or recklessly driven cars were seen. Many travelers have spotted white, transparent, amorphous clouds floating in the roadbed or on the shoulder that could not be explained by weather conditions. In many cases, witnesses report apparitions that were clearly identifiable as bloodied people standing or laying by the road.

Over a five-year period, I interviewed nine people who nearly lost control of their vehicle when a ghost appeared in the backseat of their car. Most of these witnesses noticed bizarre, unexplained odors inside the car before seeing lifelike beings or transparent apparitions. One witness, a deputy sheriff trained in accident investigation, told me the odor he detected was that of burned flesh.

Hundreds of sightings have occurred on either side of Highway 17, but they are more frequent on the northbound side. Those lanes are traveled by people who are tired from a long day in the sun at the Santa Cruz beach. California Highway Patrol records indicate that drivers operating under the influence of alcohol are major contributors to this highway's reputation as Blood Alley.

GHOSTS OF THE DIGGERS

Santa Cruz Mountain Tunnels
Glenwood Tunnel at Laurel Tunnel and Wright Tunnel
Laurel Road at Schulties Road
Santa Cruz Mountains

Each hour, thousands of people cross the Santa Cruz Mountains on Highway 17, traveling between Bay Area cities and the beaches of Monterey Bay completely unaware that they are passing over an extensive series of 19th-century train tunnels. They are also unaware the tunnels under Highway 17 now serve as tombs for miners killed in cave-ins and gas explosions. Well-trained bicyclists who ride the winding back roads of the Santa Cruz Mountains occasionally spot the sealed entrance to one of these tunnels or remnants of a train bridge, but most are concealed from view, hidden by overgrown brush or the shade of a tall redwood. Even some locals can't tell you exactly where the tunnels are located, but the area's ghost hunters can direct you to those that are haunted.

In the 1870s, travel between the cities of the south Bay Area and Monterey Bay was arduous and often dangerous. Stagecoaches negotiated narrow, muddy roads between Los Gatos and Santa Cruz, taking two days to make the trip. Seeing the economic potential of

Throughout the Santa Cruz Mountains, remnants of eight railroad tunnels can be found. During construction of Laurel Tunnel, several workers died from a massive explosion and cave-in.

resorts and recreational centers on Monterey Bay, San Francisco capitalists James Fair and Alfred E. Davis planned a railroad line that would carry visitors and freight across the Sana Cruz Mountains. Since no engine existed that could pull heavy cars over the 1,800-foot summit, Fair and Davis ordered the construction of a series of eight tunnels, some more than 2.5 miles long. Hundreds of laborers, mostly Chinese, were employed in the dangerous work. To support them, several villages sprang up, composed of bunkhouses, company stores, shanties, and barrooms. Today, only a few foundations and piles of wood remain to mark the places where these villages once stood.

In 1879, during construction of the Wright Tunnel and the Laurel Tunnel, two massive gas explosions killed 33 miners and injured more than 100. Most of the victims were buried in graves near the tunnel villages. However, since the victims' bodies were literally blown apart, some of the remains are still entombed in the tunnels under Highway 17.

The ghosts of these workers may have started appearing soon after death, but there is no credible report of a sighting until January 16, 1890. An article appeared in a local newspaper in which an area resident recounted his encounter with the ghosts of more than 30 miners as they emerged from the mouth of Wright Tunnel. Since that sighting, the sealed tunnels of the Santa Cruz Mountains have been hot spots for paranormal investigators. More recently, ghost hunters have detected bizarre light anomalies, including orbs, near tunnel entrances. Occasional sightings of apparitions occur, but audio phenomenon is far more common. EVP practitioners pick up moaning, screams, sobbing, and crashing sounds.

Some of the paranormal phenomena detected near these tunnels may be the result of a tragic accident that occurred on May 23, 1880. An excursion train left the tracks at high speed and crashed into the redwoods. Fifteen people lost their lives while more than 50 were seriously injured.

Today, ghost hunters can board the Mountain Charlie Railroad in Felton and ride through the majestic stands of redwoods and train tunnels built in the 20th century. This trip offers an opportunity to get off the train for an hour to hike the mountains, searching for ghosts of the 1880 train accident, before boarding the next train that passes. If you plan to drive into the mountains in search of the tunnels, study topographic and historical maps carefully. Many of the roads are narrow, poorly maintained, cling to steep mountainsides, and may be hazardous in bad weather. (See www.lakata.org/arch/santacruztunnels/ for a useful map.)

Other places to hunt ghosts:

GHOST OF THE SUICIDE TEACHER

Lincoln Adelaida School
9000 Chimney Rock Road
Latitude: 35.668060
Longitude: -120.854720
Near Paso Robles 93446

This schoolhouse now sits empty on private land, but it is open for tours on special occasions. Check with the local historical association for dates and times. Built around 1900, the location has a tragic history associated with it, plus bizarre myths and superstitions. It has been reported that a teacher, despondent over the death of her fiancé in the local mercury mine, hanged herself one evening from the schoolhouse ceiling. Several children discovered her body as they arrived for class in the morning. The ghost of this tragic figure has been spotted sitting in a chair inside the classroom. According to local legend, she also causes car engines to stall when frightened teenagers try to leave the place.

GHOSTS OF THE FATHER AND DAUGHTER

Miller Mansion Ruins
Mount Madonna Park
7850 Pole Line Road
Watsonville 95076
408-842-2341

Within 10 years of arriving in California with only five dollars in his pocket, Heinrick Kreiser (1827-1916) had changed his name to Henry Miller and become one of the state's richest men. His domain included one million acres of land and more than one million head of cattle. His summer retreat included 13,000 acres, which is now open to the public as Mount Madonna State Park. The ruins of Kreiser's summer mansion are haunted by his ghost and that of his daughter, Sarah Alice Miller. Nicknamed Gussie, eight-year-old Sarah died on June 13, 1879, when her galloping horse's foreleg was caught in a gopher hole. The ghost of little Gussie has been seen riding the trails of Mount Madonna. Visitors have also reported seeing a little girl, wearing a frilly white dress, walking along the roadside at night. Sarah's father nicknamed her Gussie because of her love of "gussying up" in frilly dresses.

MISSION SANTA INEZ

1760 Mission Drive
Solvang 93464
805-688-4815

Founded in 1804 as a buffer between the Spanish coastal establishments at Santa Barbara and La Purisima and the warlike Tulare Indian tribes to the northeast, Mission Santa Inez is best known for its pivotal role in the Indian revolt of 1824. Pushed to their limits by abusive soldiers, the Indians attacked the mission and set several buildings on fire. Lasting several months, the revolt took the lives of two Indians and injured several soldiers. Like all Spanish missions in California, many of the Indian converts, called neophytes, were buried near the church in unmarked graves. Ghost hunters using dowsing rods have detected several anomalies around the restored mission that may indicate mass graves. These would be good places for EVP investigation.

MISSION NUESTRA SENORA DE LA SOLEDAD

36641 Fort Romie Road
Soledad 93960
831-678-2586
www.missiontour.org/soledad/index.htm

Dedicated to the "Solitude of Most Holy Mary," the Mission Nuestra Senora de la Soledad was not the peaceful oasis suggested by its name. Founded by Father Lasuen on October 9, 1791, the place was destroyed twice by flooding from the nearby Salinas River. During reconstruction in 1832, a third flood damaged the mission's fields and agricultural infrastructure so badly that it never recovered. In addition to these calamities, *padres* who served there complained of the inhospitable climate. The misery of long hot summers was matched by freezing winter nights, causing many clergy to suffer from poor health. As many as 30 priests were assigned to Mission Soledad in a span of five decades. Many of them were buried in the mission graveyard, but their spirits are not at rest. Apparitions of hooded figures are often spotted walking the grounds. Some of these ghosts chant in Spanish and create an odor of rotting leather.

LA CASA ROSA

107 Third Street
San Juan Bautista 95045
831-623-4563

Located only a few short blocks from the historic plaza and Mission San Juan Bautista, this quaint watering hole has a ghost that smokes cigarettes. Patrons often detect the telltale odor when no one in the place is smoking. The smell of smoke is usually limited to a very small area, as if the odor came from the clothing of an unseen person who happened to be a smoker. Sensitives who have visited La Casa Rosa believe the invisible smoker is a prostitute who used to work in the building and enjoy a drink and a smoke between customers.

MARIPOSA HOUSE RESTAURANT

37 Mariposa Street
San Juan Bautista 95045
831-623-4666

This popular restaurant occupies an 1892 vintage Victorian house, which probably explains why the place is haunted. A ghost named Rachel creates cool breezes and the sound of footsteps going up and down the stairs. Her partial apparition, with long, dark hair, has been spotted wearing a red dress. It is believed that Rachel lived and died in the house early in the 20th century, when it was located on the corner of Third and Mariposa. In 1972, it was moved to its present location. Local history buffs believe Rachel died at the age of 20 from peritonitis after giving birth to her only child.

Other San Juan hot spots for ghosts:

San Juan Bautista 95045

Almost every building in San Juan Bautista has a ghost story attached to it. Many locals have told some fascinating stories about ghosts that have driven residents from their homes or frightened people who walk the town's quaint streets in the evening. A swing at Abbe Park, on Muckelemi Street, moves as if an invisible person were swinging. Transparent, partial apparitions of cowboys have walked through La Problanita Mexican Restaurant on Third Street. A phantom stagecoach has been reported at the end of Washington Street between Second and El Camino Real. In keeping with the objective of this book, these places are accessible to the general public. If you take the time to inquire of locals about their experiences with paranormal activity, you may get an invitation to visit one of the many haunted private homes or offices in town.

Sighting Report Form

GENERAL INSTRUCTIONS

Photocopy and enlarge the form on the next page to a standard 8.5 x 11 inch format. This form should be completed immediately after a sighting. If the ghost hunt is performed by a group, a designated leader should assume the role of reporter. The reporter is responsible for completing this form.

The reporter and each witness should make a statement, either audio or written, describing in full their experience at the site. Date, sign, and label these statements with a reference number identical to the report number on the sighting report form. Attach the statements to the report form.

SIGHTING REPORT

SITE NAME _____ REPORT # _____

LOCATION _____ DATE: _____

TIME: _____

REPORTER _____ SITE # _____

WITNESSES _____
_____
_____

DESCRIPTION OF APPARITION: _____

temperature change	[] YES	[] NO
auditory phenomena	[] YES	[] NO
telekinesis	[] YES	[] NO
visual phenomena	[] YES	[] NO
other phenomena	[] YES	[] NO

Description: _____
_____

Use the reverse side for diagrams, maps, and drawings.
SPECIFIC LOCATION WITHIN SITE: _____
_____

PREVIOUS SIGHTINGS AT THIS SITE?:   [] YES   [] NO
Reference: _____ _____
Summary: ___ _____

RECORDS:
audio	[] YES	[] NO	Ref. No. _____
video	[] YES	[] NO	Ref. No. _____
photo	[] YES	[] NO	Ref. No. _____

Summary of records: _____
Disposition of records: _____

WITNESS STATEMENTS—Summary: _____
_____

audio	[] YES	[] NO
written	[] YES	[] NO

Disposition of statements: _____
_____

Suggested Reading

BOOKS

Allison, Ross and Joe Teeples. *Ghostology 101: Becoming a Ghost Hunter.* Seattle, WA: AuthorHouse, 2005.

Auerbach, Loyd. *ESP, Hauntings, and Poltergeists.* New York: Warner Books, 1986.

————. *Ghost Hunting: How to Investigate the Paranormal.* Oakland, CA: Ronin Publishing, 2004.

Belanger, Jeff. *The World's Most Haunted Places.* Franklin Lakes, NJ: Career Press, 2004.

Dwyer, Jeff. *Ghost Hunter's Guide to Los Angeles.* Gretna, LA: Pelican Publishing, 2007.

————. *Ghost Hunter's Guide to New Orleans.* Gretna, LA: Pelican Publishing, 2007.

————. *Ghost Hunter's Guide to Seattle and Puget Sound.* Gretna, LA: Pelican Publishing, 2008.

————. *Ghost Hunter's Guide to the San Francisco Bay Area.* Gretna, LA: Pelican Publishing, 2005.

Hauck, Dennis William. *Haunted Places: The National Directory.* New York: Penguin Group, 2002.

Hawes, Jason, Grant Wilson, and Michael Jan Friedman. *Ghost Hunting: True Stories of Unexplained Phenomena from the Atlantic Paranormal Society.* New York: Pocket Publishers, 2007.

Holzer, Hans. *Ghosts I've Met.* Chicago: Barnes & Noble Books, 2005.

Juliano, Dave. *Ghost Research 101: Investigating Haunted Homes.* Mount Holly, NJ: In the Shadows Publishing, 2005.

Lankford, Andrea. *Haunted Hikes: Spine-tingling Tales and Trails from North America's National Parks.* Santa Monica, CA: Santa Monica Press, 2006.

Ramsland, Katherine. *Ghost: Investigating the Other Side.* New York: St. Martin's Press, 2001.

Reinstedt, Randall. *California Ghost Notes.* Carmel, CA: Ghost Town Publications, 2000.

————. *Ghost Notes: Haunted Happenings on California's Historic Monterey Peninsula.* Carmel, CA: Ghost Town Publications, 1991.

————. *Ghost Tales and Mysterious Happenings of Old Monterey.* Carmel, CA: Ghost Town Publications, 1977.

Senate, Richard. *Ghosts of the Haunted Coast.* Channel Islands, CA: Pathfinder Publishing, 1999.

————. *The Haunted Southland.* Ventura, CA: Charon Press, 1994.

Smith, Barbara. *Ghost Stories of California.* Renton, WA: Lone Pine Publishing, 2000.

Southall, R. H. *How to be a Ghost Hunter.* Woodbury, MN: Llewellyn Publications, 2003.

Steiger, Brad. *Real Ghosts, Restless Spirits, and Haunted Places.* Detroit: Visible Ink Press, 2003.

Sweet, Lenore. *How to Photograph the Paranormal.* Charlottesville, VA: Hampton Roads Publishing, 2004.

Taylor, Troy. *Ghost Hunter's Guidebook.* Alton, IL: Whitechapel Productions Press, 1999.

————. *Ghost Hunter's Guidebook: The Essential Guide to Investigating Ghosts and Hauntings.* Alton, IL: White Chapel Productions, 2007.

Winer, Richard. *Ghost Ship: True Stories of Nautical Nightmares, Hauntings and Disasters.* New York: Berkeley Publishing Group, 2000.

Winkowski, Mary Ann. *When Ghosts Speak: Understanding the World of Earthbound Spirits.* New York: Grand Central Publishing, 2007.

Wlodarski, Robert, and Anne Wlodarski. *California Hauntspitality.* Alton, IL: White Chapel Productions Press, 2002.

Van Praagh, James. *Ghosts Among Us: Uncovering the Truth about the Other Side.* New York: HarperOne, 2008.

ARTICLES

Barrett, Greg. "Can the Living Talk to the Dead? Psychics Say They Connect with the Other World, but Skeptics Respond: 'Prove It.'" *USA Today,* 20 June 2001.

Cadden, Mary. "Get Spooked on a Walking Tour." *USA Today,* 17 October 2003.

Calvan, Bobby Caina. "Ghost of a Chance." *Sacramento Bee,* 22 January 2008.

Clark, Jayne. "10 Great Places to Get Spooked by Your Surroundings." *USA Today,* 26 October 2007.

Delsol, Christine. "Historic Ghosts of Old Monterey." *San Francisco Chronicle,* 14 October 2007.

Giovannetti, Joe. "Crossing Over: Ghost Hunter Knows Things That Go Bump in the Night." *Fairfield (CA) Daily Republic,* 18 October 2007.

Guzman, Isaiah. "Ghostbusters Scour Brookdale Lodge." *Santa Cruz Sentinel,* 19 January 2008.

Hill, Angela. "Paranormal Experts Say It's Not All Funny." *Oakland (CA) Tribune,* 18 October 2002.

Massingill, T. "Business of Ghost Busting." *Contra Costa Times,* 8 October 2000.

McManis, Sam. "The X-Files of Contra Costa/Lloyd Auerbach Shares Tales from the Dark Side." *San Francisco Chronicle,* 30 October 1998.

Moran, Gwen. "Real-Life Ghost Busters." *USA Weekend,* 31 October 2004.

Nowacki, Kim. "Here's How Real Ghost-Hunters Work." *Yakima Herald-Republic,* 20 October 2003.

Parker, Ann. "Ghost Bust'er." *Santa Cruz Sentinel,* 14 May 2006.

———. "Spirited Dining at the Brookdale Lodge." *Santa Cruz Sentinel,* 14 September 2005.

———. "Spirited Goings-on in Scottish Pub." *Santa Cruz Sentinel,* 14 May 2006.

Ravn, Karen. "Looking for Ghosts in Monterey. *Monterey County Herald,* 31 October 2006.

Schoolmeester, Ron. "10 Great Places to Go on a Haunted Hike." *USA Today,* 28 July 2006.

Sichelman, Lew. "Plenty of Spooky Sites around the Nation." *San Francisco Chronicle,* 28 October 2007.

———. "When a Cemetery Could Be Your Next-Door Neighbor. *San Francisco Chronicle,* 26 October 2008.

Speckert, Corinne. "Fabled Brookdale Lodge Holds 'Spirits' Tour." *Santa Cruz Sentinel,* 15 July 2008.

APPENDIX C

Organizations

You may contact these organizations to report ghost phenomena, obtain advice, or arrange for an investigation of a haunting. Many of these organizations conduct conferences, offer training, or list educational opportunities for those seeking to become paranormal investigators.

American Society for Psychical Research
5 West 73rd Street
New York, NY 10023
212-799-5050

Berkeley Psychic Institute
2436 Hastings Street
Berkeley, CA 94704
510-548-8020

Central Coast Paranormal Investigators
Web site: www.ccpinvestigators.com

Committee for Scientific Investigations of Claims of the Paranormal
1203 Kensington Avenue
Buffalo, NY 14215

Department of Psychology
Jordan Hall, Building 420
Stanford University
Stanford, CA 94305
Division of Parapsychology
Box 152, Medical Center
Charlottesville, VA 22908

Ghost Trackers
P.O. Box 89
Santa Clara, CA 95052
408-244-8331
E-mail: ghosttrackers@yahoo.com
Web site: www.ghost-trackers.org

Institute for Parapsychology
P.O. Box 6847
College Station
Durham, NC 27708

International Society for Paranormal Research
4712 Admiralty Way
Marina del Rey, CA 90292

Office of Paranormal Investigations
JFK University
12 Altarinda Road
Orinda, CA 94563
415-249-9275

Orange County Society for Psychic Research
Web site: www.ocspr.org

San Diego Paranormal Research Project
E-mail: info@sdparanormal.com
Web site: www.sdparanormal.com

Society for Psychical Research
Eleanor O'Keffe, secretary
49 Marloes Road
Kensington, London W8 6LA
+02-07-937-8984

Southern California Society for Psychical Research
269 South Arden Boulevard
Los Angeles, CA 90004

Films, DVDs, and Videos

Fictional films may provide you with information that will assist you in preparing for a ghost hunt. This assistance ranges from putting you in the proper mood for ghost hunting to useful techniques for exploring haunted places. Some films, especially documentaries, may provide information about the nature of ghostly activity.

America's Most Haunted Inns (2004). Documentary. Directed by Robert Child.
America's Most Haunted Town (2001). Documentary. Directed by Robert Child.
Beyond Belief: Investigation into the Paranormal (2006). Documentary.
Cemetery Man (1994). Directed by Michele Soavi, starring Rupert Everett and Francois Hadji-Lazaro.
City of Angels (1998). Directed by Brad Silberling, starring Nicolas Cage and Meg Ryan.
Dragonfly (2002). Directed by Tom Shadyac, starring Kevin Costner and Kathy Bates.
The Entity (1983). Directed by Sidney J. Furie, starring Barbara Hershey and Ron Silver.
Ghost of Flight 409 (1987, made for TV). Directed by Steven Hilliard Stern, starring Ernest Borgnine and Kim Bassinger.
Ghost Story (1981). Directed by John Irvin, starring Fred Astaire and Melvyn Douglas.
Ghost Stories, Volume 1 (1997). Documentary hosted by Patrick McNee.
Ghost Stories, Volume 2 (1997). Documentary hosted by Patrick McNee.
Haunted (1995). Directed by Lewis Gilbert, starring Aidan Quinn and Kate Beckinsale.
Haunted History (2002). History Channel Home Video.
The Haunting (1999). Directed by Jan De Bont, starring Liam Neeson and Catherine Zeta-Jones.
Haunting across America (2001). Documentary hosted by Michael Dorn.

The Haunting of Molly Hartley (2008). Directed by Mickey Liddell, starring Haley Bennett and Jake Weber.

The Haunting of Seacliff Inn (1995). Directed by Walter Klenhard, starring Ally Sheedy and William R. Moses.

Hollywood Ghosts & Gravesites (2003). Documentary.

The ISPR Investigates Ghosts of England and Belgrave Hall (2001). Documentary.

Living With the Dead (2000). Directed by Stephen Gyllenhaal, starring Ted Danson and Mary Steenburgen.

Mysterious Forces Beyond, Volume 2: Death and Paranormal (2002). Documentary.

The Others (2001). Directed by Alejandro Amenabar, starring Nicole Kidman and Christopher Eccleston.

Poltergeist (1982). Directed by Tobe Hooper, starring JoBeth Williams and Craig T. Nelson.

Poltergeist II: The Other Side (1986). Directed by Brian Gibson, starring JoBeth Williams and Craig T. Nelson.

Restless Spirits (1999). Directed by David Wellington, starring Lothaire Bluteau and Marsha Mason.

Sightings: Heartland Ghost (2002). Directed by Brian Trenchard-Smith, starring Randy Birch and Beau Bridges.

The Sixth Sense (1999). Directed by M. Night Shyamalan, starring Bruce Willis and Haley Joel Osment.

Thir13en Ghosts (2001). Directed by Steve Beck, starring Tony Shalhoub.

White Noise (2005). Directed by Geoffrey Sax, starring Michael Keaton.

1408 (2007). Directed by Mikael Hafstrom. Starring John Cusack and Samuel L. Jackson.

The following movies are not about ghosts, but they are worth watching before visiting California's haunted coast. They provide a sneak preview of some of the scenery and a bit of local culture. Go to www.filmmonterey.org to see a complete list of movies filmed in the Monterey area.

Cannery Row (1982). Directed by David S. Ward, starring Nick Nolte and Debra Winger. Filmed in Pacific Grove.

I Know Who Killed Me (2007). Directed by Chris Silverston, starring Lindsay Lohan. Filmed in Morro Bay.

Play Misty for Me (1971). Directed by Clint Eastwood, starring Clint Eastwood and Jessica Walter. Filmed in Carmel and Monterey.

Sudden Impact (1983). Directed by Clint Eastwood, starring Clint Eastwood and Sandra Locke. Filmed in Santa Cruz.

Turner and Hooch (1989). Directed by Roger Spottiswoode, starring Tom Hanks and Mare Winningham. Filmed in Pacific Grove.

Internet Resources

www.aaevp.com. The American Association for Electronic Voice Phenomena, founded by Sarah Estep, offers advice, and opportunities to learn new EVCP techniques.

www.californiahistoricalsociety.org/. This official site of the California Historical Society offers publications and several links to help ghost hunters research specific events, historical figures, or historic sites.

www.californiahistory.com/. This site offers several articles about California history, which serve as a useful orientation for visitors from distant parts of the United States. E-mail: cahist@aol.com.

www.csgr.us/. Located in Corona, California, this group focuses on ghost towns.

www.ghosthunter.com. Web site of ghost hunter and lecturer Patti Starr.

www.ghostresearch.com. Web site for information about ghost hunting methods and equipment and on-going investigations.

www.ghostresearch.org. Ghost Research Society was established in 1971 as a clearinghouse for reports of paranormal activity. Members research homes and businesses and analyze photographs and audio and video recordings to establish authenticity. This society is headed by well-known ghost researcher Dale Kaczmarek.

www.ghost-stalker.com. Richard Senate is a well-known author, lecturer, and ghost investigator who focuses mainly on southern California locations.

www.ghoststore.net. This is an online catalog listing a vast array of ghost-hunting equipment available for purchase.

www.ghosttowns.com. Informative Web site that gives detailed information about ghost towns in the U.S. and Canada.

www.ghost-trackers.org. Ghost Trackers are a professional research group based in the San Francisco Bay Area. Among their members are scientists and expert technicians. E-mail: ghostttrackers@yahoo.com.

www.ghostweb.com. International Ghost Hunters Society, headed by Drs. Sharon Gill and Dave Oester, researches spirits to produce evidence of life after death. The society offers a home-study certification for paranormal investigators. Membership exceeds 15,000.

www.hollowhill.com. A ghost information Web site that displays reports, photographs, eye-witness accounts, location information, and ghost-hunting techniques.

www.hpiparanormal.net. Haunted and Paranormal Investigations International is a highly active group of ghost hunters who have considerable experience with Sacramento-area and Gold Rush country spirits. E-mail: ghost@snmproductionsco.com.

www.ispr.net/home.html. International Society for Paranormal Research, headed by Dr. Larry Montz, conducts ghost expeditions, provides the media with expert opinions on paranormal issues, and lists classes and products of interest to ghost hunters.

www.jeffdwyer.com. Web site of paranormal investigator, ghost hunter, and writer Jeff Dwyer.

www.mindreader.com. Office of Paranormal Investigations. Directed by internationally known author and researcher Loyd Auerbach, the office investigates a variety of paranormal activity for a fee.

www.nationalghosthunters.com/investigations.html. Official Web site of the National Ghost Hunters Society. This organization of psychics and mediums helps people solve their ghost problems.

www.pacificparanormal.com. This southern California-based nonprofit organization specializes in the San Diego region, but its members travel all over California to assist clients.

www.paranormality.com/ghost_hunting_equipment.shtml. The site lists high-tech equipment useful in paranormal investigations.

www.prairieghosts.com/ghost_hunt.html. Official Web site of the American Ghost Society, founded by ghost researchers Troy and Amy Taylor. This site provides information about ghost research, paranormal investigations, and books written by Troy Taylor.

www.preservationnation.org/travel-and-sites/travel/historic-hotels.html. Historic hotels of America are detailed here.

www.psiapplications.com. PSI is a northern California organization dedicated to the investigation and documentation of anomalous events, including the paranormal.

www.sjvparanormal.com. The San Joaquin Valley Research covers the Central Valley and parts of northern California.

www.sonomaspirit.com. Headed by EVP expert Jackie Ganiy, this organization maintains a Web site that serves as a great research utility.

www.the-atlantic-paranormal-society.com. Official Web site of the Atlantic Paranormal Society (TAPS). This group of ghost investigators gained famed through the Syfy Channel's *Ghost Hunters.* The organization has more than 50 groups throughout the U.S. and has demonstrated excellence and discretion in its investigations of the paranormal.

www.theshadowlands.net/ghost. Directory of reports of unsubstantiated hauntings and other paranormal events organized by state. This is a good Web site for finding places that might be hot spots for ghostly activity.

www.venturahaunts.com. This group specializes in the southern California coastal region.

www.warrens.net/. The New England Society for Psychic Research, the official Web site for famed researchers and demonologists Ed and Lorraine Warren.

APPENDIX F

Special Tours and Events

Big Sur Lighthouse Tour: Every Saturday and Sunday, docents guide visitors on a 2- to 3-hour tour of the historic lighthouse that has marked the Big Sur headland since 1889. The history of lighthouse keepers and tragic shipwrecks is presented. Adults $5.00, children $3.00. Saturdays at 10:00 A.M. and 2:00 P.M.; Sundays at 2:00 P.M. 831-625-4419.

Borromeo del Rio Carmelo Mission: This walking tour reveals the fascinating history of one of California's most famous missions. Features include the grave of Father Junipero Serra and the mission graveyard. 3080 Rio Road, Carmel. 831-624-1271.

Candlelight Tour of the Old Adobe with Ghost Stories: Every October, the Rios-Caledonia Adobe in San Miguel hosts this event to start the Halloween season. Local historians and docents tell stories of hauntings and other legends. 805-467-3357. www.rios-caledoniaadobe.org/.

Ghost Tours of Big Sur Lighthouse: This tour is offered at 5:15 P.M. the weekend before Halloween. Guests enjoy a spectacular sunset over the ocean while warming-up with hearty refreshments. Professional actor and storyteller Kevin Hanstick recounts real stories of ghost sightings and poltergeist activity that have occurred at the 1879-vintage lighthouse. $50.00 per person. 408-649-7139 or e-mail cclk@pointsur.org.

Ghost Trolley of Old Monterey: This 90-minute trolley tour led by longtime residents and historians will bring you face to face with Monterey's spirit community. Guides will share the latest ghost stories and offer opportunities for guests to photograph haunted locations. Adults $28.00, children $9.00. 8:00 P.M. Wednesday through Saturday. Meet at 527 Hartnell Street. 831-624-1700.

Hearst Castle at San Simeon: The state of California operates five guided public tours of this amazing 165-room castle and on 127-acre grounds every day except Thanksgiving, Christmas, and New Year's. Daytime tours are 1 hour and 45 minutes; evening tours are 2 hours and 10 minutes. Adults $24.00, children $12.00. 800-444-4445.

Historic Walking Tour of Carmel: This 90-minute guided tour focuses on the history of Carmel and some of its most famous residents. Tour starts at 9:30 A.M. on the first Saturday of each month. $10.00 donation to Carmel Heritage Society. 831-624-4447.

Monterey Walking Path of History: This tour covers two miles and includes many of Monterey's oldest structures, including the Stevenson House, the Cooper-Molera Adobe, and the Custom House. Free. 831-649-7118.

Pacific Grove Victorian Home Tour: This docent-led tour of historic homes, bed and breakfast inns, and churches provide ghosts hunters with rare opportunities to visit the interiors of some of the oldest structures in town. October weekends. 831-373-3304. www.pacificgrove.org.

San Juan Bautista State Historic Park: This guided tour for 10 to 25 guests examines buildings, including the Zanetta House, Plaza Stables, and Castro-Breen Adobe, and other historical remnants of the Spanish, Mexican, and early American periods in California. It also includes locations seen in Alfred Hitchcock's classic film *Vertigo.* San Juan Bautista State Park, 831-623-4881.

Santa Cruz Mountains Ghost Train: Ride an old steam engine through the towering redwoods of the coastal mountains as a narrator recounts the legend of Sleepy Hollow. This fabulous train ride takes you through spooky stands of 1,000-year-old redwoods and eerie fern grottoes. Presented the last weekend before Halloween. Roaring Camp Railroad, Felton. 831-335-4484. www.roaringcamp.com.

Stevenson House Tour: Visit the home of Robert Louis Stevenson with knowledgeable docents who may be willing to share stories of the ghosts that inhabit this place. The 45-minute tours are available Mondays and Fridays at 2:00 P.M. and Saturdays and Sundays at 10:30 A.M.

Walking Tour of Carmel: Stroll with a knowledgeable guide through hidden pathways, courtyards, and gardens in one of America's most famous towns. Learn about the arcane history of the characters and customs that make this town so unique. Two-hour tours, Tuesdays through Fridays begin at 10:00 A.M. and on Saturdays at 10:00 A.M. and 2:00 P.M. Fee varies with size of group. 831-632-2700.

Appendix G

Historical Societies and Museums

Historical societies and museums are good places to discover information about old houses and other buildings or places that figure prominently in local history. They often contain records in the form of vintage newspapers, diaries, and photographs about tragic events, such as fires, hangings, train wrecks, and earthquakes, that led to the loss of life. Old photographs and maps that are not on display for public viewing may be available to serious researchers.

Aptos Museum
7605 Old Dominion Court #B
Aptos, CA 95003
831-688-9514

Atascadero Historical Museum
6600 Lewis Avenue
Atascadero, CA 93422
805-466-8341

Big Sur Historical Society
Highway 1
Big Sur, CA 93920
831-667-2956

Boronda History Center
333 Boronda Road
Salinas, CA 93907
831-757-8085

Cambria Historical Society
Cambria, CA 93428
805-927-2891

Carmel Valley Historical Society
20 Carmel Valley Village Center
Carmel, CA 93924
831-659-5715

Colton Hall Museum
580 Pacific Street
Monterey, CA 93940
831-646-5648

Gilroy Museum
195 5th Street
Gilroy, CA 95020
408-846-0446

Guadalupe Historical Association
1005 Guadalupe Street
Guadalupe, CA 93434
805-343-5901

Historical Society of Morro Bay
1600 Preston Lane
Morro Bay, CA 93442
805-772-1058

Lompoc Museum
200 South H Street
Lompoc, CA 93436
805-736-3888

Monterey History and Maritime
    Museum
5 Custom House Plaza
Monterey, CA 93940
831-372-2608

Monterey County Historical Society
P.O. Box 3576
Salinas, CA 93912
831-757-8085

Morgan Hill Historical Museum
600 West Main Avenue
Morgan Hill, CA 95037
408-779-5755

Morgan Hill Historical Society
17860 Monterey Street
Morgan Hill, CA 95037
408-782-7191

Museum of Natural History of
    Morro Bay
20 State Park Road
Morro Bay, CA 93442
805-772-2694

Natural History Museum of Santa
    Maria
412 South McClelland Street
Santa Maria, CA 93454
805-614-0806

Pacific Grove Heritage Society
605 Laurel Avenue
Pacific Grove, CA 93950
831-372-2898

Pacific Grove Museum of Natural
    History
165 Forest Avenue
Pacific Grove, CA 93950
831-648-5716

Pajaro Valley Historical Association
332 East Beach Street
Watsonville, CA 95076
831-722-0305

Paso Robles Historical Society
2010 Riverside Avenue
Paso Robles, CA 93446
805-238-4996

Pioneer Museum
2010 Riverside Avenue
Paso Robles, CA 93446
805-239-4556

Presidio of Monterey
Corporal Ewing Road Bldg 113
Monterey, CA 93944
831-646-3456

San Luis Obispo County Historical
    Society
696 Monterey Street
San Luis Obispo, CA 93401
805-543-0638

Santa Barbara Historical Society
136 East de la Guerra Street
Santa Barbara, CA 93101
805-966-1601
www.santabarbaramuseum.com

Santa Clara County Historical and
  Genealogical Society
2635 Homestead Road
Santa Clara, CA 95051

Santa Cruz Museum of Natural
  History
1305 East Cliff Drive
Santa Cruz, CA 95062
831-420-6115

San Benito County Historical
  Society
498 5th Street
Hollister, CA 95023
831-635-335

Santa Inez Valley Historical Society
3596 Sagunto Street
Santa Inez, CA 93460
805-688-7889

Santa Maria Historical Society
616 South Broadway
Santa Maria, CA 93454
805-922-3130

South County Historical Society
P.O. Box 633
Arroyo Grande, CA 93421

Steinbeck Museum
1 Main Street
Salinas, CA 93901
831-796-3833

Stowitts Museum and Library
591 Lighthouse Avenue #20
Pacific Grove, CA 93950
831-625-4325

Surfing Museum at Lighthouse
  Point
701 West Cliff Drive
Santa Cruz, CA 95060
831-420-6289

Wings of History Aircraft Museum
12777 Murphy Avenue
San Martin, CA 95046
408-683-2290

Index